D1084904

A HISTORY OF CHAGFORD

A History of
CHAGFORD

Jane Hayter~Hames

PHILLIMORE

1981

Published by
PHILLIMORE & CO. LTD.
London and Chichester

Head Office: Shopwyke Hall,
Chichester, Sussex, England

© Jane Hayter-Hames, 1981

ISBN 0 85033 414 4

Printed and bound in Great Britain
by Billing and Sons Limited
Guildford, London, Oxford, Worcester

CONTENTS

LIST OF ILLUSTRATIONS

(between pages 48 and 49)

LIST OF FIGURES

Photography: Chris Chapman.
Map: David Ashby.
Etchings: Samuel Prout (1783-1852).

In memory of my father

INTRODUCTION

FOR ATTEMPTING a history of Chagford—ancient settlement, medieval manor, Stannary town and rural parish—I have several reasons.

Firstly, I am deeply indebted to Winifred Osborne, for asking me to complete a project for which her late husband, Francis Osborne, had spent so much of his spare time collecting material. A keen churchman, he began, early in his life, working with Miss Ethel Lega-Weekes on a translation of the early Churchwarden's Accounts. These accounts, written in 15th-centuryLatin, begin in 1480 and are among the earliest in Devon. They contain a tremendous amount of information about the life of, and changes in, the Church itself and the community in those days. It took 25 years of work in vacations to transcribe most of volume one into modern English and, after Miss Lega-Weekes' death in 1940, Frank Osborne completed the work, a labour of real love that prompted him to collect and investigate any material he could find about the history of the parish. He had planned to write the history in his retirement, and during his life he was continually called upon to answer queries on the history of the Church in particular, and also on a wide range of subjects from the parish's history. That he knew a great deal more than I can possibly know is assured; unfortunately, his death in 1964, at the age of 74, left the work unfinished. The material mainly consisted of notes, which needed collating and adding to before the history could be written. His widow, Winifred Osborne, carried on the work, verfied all the material her husband had left her, and continued to collect and sort. She kindly asked me to complete the project and I have tried to do so.

Secondly, I jumped at the opportunity out of real interest. I was born in Chagford, grew up here and, despite some ramblings, have never doubted that it is my home. I have seen some spectacular scenery, some magnificent mountains, some enormous plains, but never anything like Dartmoor. It has a special quality of intensity and freedom which is important to me. Its variety, its surprises, its wonderful colours are like nothing else. In some truly remarkable places, I have stopped to heave a sigh and wish I was on top of Meldon, with the wind in my hair.

In addition, there is no more fascinating way of learning history than to follow the story of one parish, from the beginning of time up to the present. When I discovered just how interesting, how unique, and often how colourful the history of this small place was, I became more and more involved.

Lastly, I have received much interest and encouragement from the parish and from outside. I can only suppose that there are many people who feel attached to, and interested in, the continuing story of this Dartmoor town.

I must say here that I have serious doubts about my abilities as a local historian; my Latin is negligible, and my knowledge of English history incomplete. It has had to improve and I hope that since all the facts have been checked, advice continually asked, and many histories worked through, where there is interpretation, it is not too far off the mark. History requires surprising depth of imagination without which it is dull and flat, but too much imagination can distort the known facts.

I have tried to tell the whole story, from the formation of the land up to the present time; there is no period empty of human interest, from the Old Stone Age up to the present day.

Winifred's own work, help, belief and encouragement have really written the book, but I am responsible for all that it maintains. I hope it gives a real impression of a very real story, offends nobody, pleases some, and that, since we grow out of the past, some knowledge of that past may contribute to making the future an even brighter one.

'Chaggeforde, in the dirt, oh Lord.'

ACKNOWLEDGEMENTS

The Devon Library Services, in the Records Office, the West Country Studies Library, and Exeter Library, have all given me their help in searching for the material for this book. Many thanks.

*

Thanks also to the Museums and to the Rescue Archaeologists for their help.

*

And to Chris Chapman who did heroic photography at short notice.

*

Many people encouraged me, particularly Roger Roberts; Nancy, who told me to write well; Christopher, who attacked my spelling; and Winifred, who read and corrected every chapter.

*

My ancestors trod behind me at every step. My many friends asked valuable questions and offered information. The ancient men sometimes seemed to stand at my shoulder.

*

I would like to thank, too late, the person who sited the Church and whoever built the clapper bridge at Scorhill.

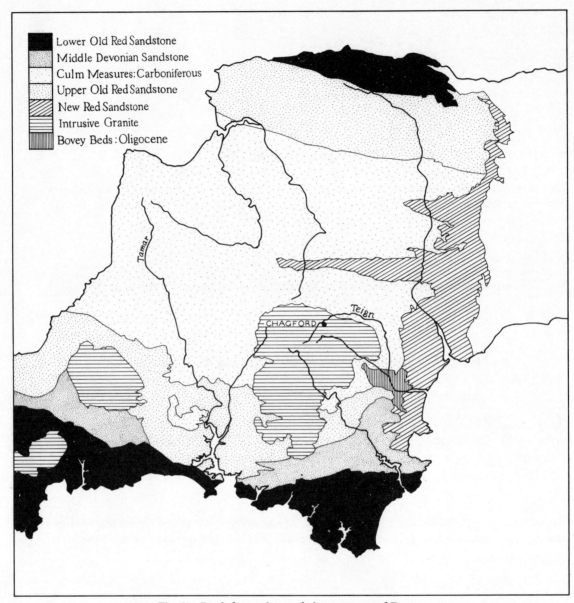

Lower Old Red Sandstone
Middle Devonian Sandstone
Culm Measures: Carboniferous
Upper Old Red Sandstone
New Red Sandstone
Intrusive Granite
Bovey Beds: Oligocene

Tamar

CHAGFORD

Teign

Fig. 1.   Rock formation and river pattern of Devon

Chapter One

THE FORMATION OF THE LAND AND ANCIENT MEN

IN EARLY DEVONIAN TIMES, that is to say 400 million years ago, the area of the earth's crust that now is Devon was part of a river flood plain. The river, long since disappeared, covered the area in sediment. Then the coast receded northwards, and Devon was submerged under a warm ocean with coral reefs and volcanic eruptions.

There it remained, collecting volcanic material, coral and mud, through the Carboniferous Era (the time of great forests and dense vegetation) until, at the end of that era, the earth's crust went into a phase of intense activity. The mountain-building period known as Armorican caused the sedimentary bed that was Devon to be lifted, folded and altered. The pressure caused by the movement changed coral into limestone, mud into shale, and the Devon sandstones were formed.

Perhaps 290 million years ago, granite pushed its way through these folded layers. The granite, hot and molten, was forced upwards from deeper inside the earth and, rising under great pressure, it forced its way through the layers of material above it. Some of this older material was burnt by the heat of the molten granite into new rock forms—this is the aureole which surrounds the moor; some particles of the older rocks were encased in the granite itself.

As it neared the surface of the earth the molten granite slowly cooled. It had risen from within, but it had also caused some pressure towards the north, which is why the highest peaks of Dartmoor are in the northern part.

While the granite cooled, fluids, gases and steam escaped from the molten material, bringing minerals in solution. Iron, lead and zinc, copper and tin found themselves deposited in layers one above the other as they cooled to their solid forms. In addition, lead may bring silver, copper brings arsenic, tin brings wolfram. There was a little gold.

After this burst of intense activity the earth's crust quietened down. Dartmoor was then mountain peaks, composed of granite core overlaid by older rocks. The covering of the granite was slowly eroded. The Jurassic period, with its great reptiles, passed. It was followed by the Cretaceous period, which was a time of warm lagoons, where small sea creatures deposited shells that would later become the chalklands of southern England. During this period, Devon was once again submerged beneath the sea, but it was beneath the water for too short a time for any extensive chalk formation, and as the Cretaceous period ended, Devon was lifted and tilted slightly to the south. At this time the present river pattern emerged.

From then on the changes in the land formation occurred by weathering and by temperature. The glaciations began, when whole areas of the earth's surface were covered in ice sheets. Between the glaciations came warm phases, when hot savanna

1

grassland covered Devon. It is generally agreed that Dartmoor was never under the ice-sheet, yet it was subjected to intense cold. Ice and frost split and removed weak material from the surface of the moor.

As the ice-sheets melted, the sea-level would rise and torrents of water removed rocks and boulders, cracked loose by the cold. The remains of the softer rocks, covering the granite, were slowly eroded and, as the surface of the granite mass became further exposed and released from the pressure of the over-lying rocks, cracks and fissures developed. Chemicals dissolved in surface water cut into the joints, deepening them, rounding and reddening the granite blocks, giving the tors the shape they have today.

Warmer weather would set in and savanna grassland would develop in Devon. Rhinoceri and hippos wandered over Devon's countryside.

The glaciations, alternating with hot periods, occupied something like two million years and it was during this period that the forms of life existing today emerged. The last of the glaciations melted away about 9,000 years ago and, by then, early man was already about his business.

At that time the south-west of England was an isolated region. Surrounded by sea on all but one side, its narrow land passage to southern England was blocked by the Somerset levels, that long flat area of Somerset which then was marsh and fen. To the north rose the Quantocks and Mendips, to the south the Blackdown Hills. The south-west was effectively isolated.

Devon was composed of two very different types of land, with the granite mass of Dartmoor firmly between. North Devon was carboniferous clay, giving thick forest and dense damp undergrowth. Southern Devon was sandstone and was also completely wooded, but it was better drained and its undergrowth limited. Between them the granite outcrop rose to well over 2,000 feet above sea level, with a thin soil cover and, as yet, no peat. As the climate became warmer, some tree cover emerged on the moor: hazel, oak and elm, but the thin soil and prevailing winds meant that the trees were always sparse and stunted.

This was the land the early man inhabited. Above the wooded valleys of the lower slopes, and the forests of the low-lying areas, the open hillsides of Dartmoor supported a variety of wild life, and among them, man.

Out of the southern edge of Whitehorse Hill, the North Teign rises, flows to the east around the base of the hill, and falls 700 feet,to where it meets the Walla Brook at Scorhill. From there it tumbles down another 400 feet to Leigh Bridge.

The South Teign rises in two places, one tributary below Sittaford Tor, the other directly west of Hurston Ridge. They meet at Fernworthy and from there the South Teign drops 600 feet to meet the North Teign at Leigh Bridge. The river runs quickly to the edge of the granite and then makes its spectacular way through the Teign Gorge, a valley it cut for itself towards the end of the glacial period. At this point it enters the carboniferous rocks that make the land of North Devon.

The town of Chagford stands on a gentle slope to the south-west of the River Teign, below the steep rise of Meldon and the higher moor, sheltered just a little from the prevailing winds, washed by the rain from the Atlantic, and cut off to the north and east by the carboniferous ridge surrounding the Teign Gorge.

Seven thousand years ago, that is to say about 5,000 B.C., the Teign valley was completely wooded. The scantier tree cover the moor supported was a more natural environment for Early Stone Age hunters. At what time they first emerged on the warm upland slopes is unknown. They hunted game with rough stone weapons and perhaps descended sometimes to the coast to fish. The climate was benevolent and caves probably provided what shelter they required.

Between 3,500 and 3,000 B.C. a new type of man arrived in Devon. Migrating up through western France, they apparently had sufficient knowledge of boats to cross the Channel to the south coast of Devon. Known as the Neolithic peoples, they had learned greater skills than the Early Stone Age hunters. They had flint tools, and made pottery. They knew how to manage cattle and sheep, and they cultivated grain. It was this last feature that made them settlers, unlike the nomadic hunters. They tended to settle around spring heads, and 16 small settlements of this type have been found at East and West Week and the Goosefords, south-west of Whiddon Down.

Flint was not found in the south-west, and apparently the Neolithic peoples would travel by sea to Dorset, from there passing up the Avon to Salisbury Plain, or crossing the Bristol Channel to South Wales and so to the Cotswolds. In this way they could trade with their neighbours and perhaps exchange new ideas and developments with them.

It seems to be during this period that a burial ritual developed in which the cremated remains were buried in urns. Spinster's Rock, one of the few cromlechs of its kind in the south-west, is said to date from this time and may have contained burial urns and even have been covered by a barrow. It has also been suggested that the cromlechs were built over underground water or force lines, capable of being demonstrated by water diviners. What our early ancestors thought and believed is unknown, but if they were capable of discovering force lines inherent in the structure of the earth and water-courses running beneath its surface, they may have wished to place their monuments on them and, possibly, bury the remains of their dead in the same way.

When the first archaeologists mapped Spinster's Rock, it was surrounded by a system of stone circles and rows, which have now disappeared. These were probably the addition of later builders, but may have been an extension of the original idea.

The climate began to deteriorate and it became colder. The tree cover on Dartmoor decreased and the peat began to form. Around 2,000 B.C. a new group of people appeared in the south-west. They probably moved into the area from Wessex and from Wales, and concentrated themselves on Dartmoor and Land's End. These are the people known to archaeologists as the Beaker People, from the distinctive style of their pottery, an example of which has been found at Chagford.

They brought with them something far more revolutionary than their pottery, and that was their knowledge of metals: they worked copper. The beginnings of the Bronze Age had dawned.

These people were supreme builders. Although in many cases they may have taken over older sites and elaborated on them, it seems that it was they who were primarily responsible for the building of the stone circles, stone rows and the first of the kistvaens and cairns that cover so much of Dartmoor. Some of their building shows strong resemblance to that of southern England and the rest of the British Isles, but the stone rows are unique to Dartmoor.

The Teign Valley contains two of the finest of their circles, the single circle at Scorhill, near the Walla Brook, and the double circles of the Grey Wethers, near the rising of the South Teign. There is a fine stone row at Hurston Ridge, and a complex of rows on Shovel Down and parts of others are found on the slopes above both North and South Teign.

The circles are especially lovely. Standing both on gentle slopes, they are surprisingly distinct from long distances, and today, for walkers over the moor, they can be useful landmarks in a continually changing landscape.

Investigation of their siting and layout suggests that they were planned along complex geometrical patterns and that they showed sometimes the rising, sometimes the setting, of the sun, the moon, and of certain bright stars. This probably accounts for their siting, for they would be placed where the horizon is far enough in the distance to get a clear siting.

The accuracy with which the cumbersome stones were laid out and the precision of the readings implies both a fine mathematical skill and a sophisticated calendar. Agricultural people are naturally more dependent than hunters not only on the changing seasons, but also on climatic and seasonal differences that might be associated with the changing position of the earth in relation to the heavens. There is also a suggestion in these monuments of an attitude we have yet to absorb, which is of a ritual and religious significance. A similarity of the great stone rings at Avebury suggests a similar culture to that of Salisbury Plain, and the worship of a fertile goddess, the Queen of Nature.

Walking over the moorland slopes of the Teign Valley, looking for Early Bronze Age sites marked on the map, I have found the stone rows, standing stones, stone circles and cairns do construct an easy system of sitings. It is a feature of Dartmoor that the tops of the hills are rounded off in a way that obscures the summit from the lower slopes, the valleys can be marshy and treacherous, and although from high ground one can see clearly the route to follow to the next hilltop, descending towards the valleys often obscures directions.

Scorhill Circle is visible from quite long distances, and before the afforestation of Fernworthy, the Grey Wethers must have been equally visible. The stone rows and circles have given me helpful directions in following the path of least resistance from ridge to ridge, and I can only suggest that this may have been at least a part of their original function.

Apart from the circles and rows, there are any number of cairns and kistvaens in the Teign Valley and on its higher slopes. They seem to have contained single burial urns and sometimes some burial goods, such as tools or some precious object. The cairn on Water Hill contained a kistvaen (a small stone chamber) and there are kistvaens at Thornworthy, Shovel Down, and on the banks of the South Teign. In some of these were found cremation urns, noticeably in a ruined cairn on Hurston Ridge, several contained flint tools, and in a kistvaen at Fernworthy there was a horn button.

The period of the Beaker people merged into the full Bronze Age by about 1,500 B.C. The knowledge of bronze working, a combination of copper and tin, crept into the area from the Mediterranean and brought new people to the south-west. Cornish tin was exported to Wessex and to other parts of Europe. Irish and Mediterranean traders came looking for the precious metal and finds of beads, tools and other ornaments of Mediterranean origin suggest that some of the traders found their way to Dartmoor.

With improved tools, living standards improved. The population seems to have increased and, although many of the monuments of an older inspiration, circles, rows and kistvaens, continued to be built or added to throughout the Bronze Age, other building was undertaken.

The native peoples, along with some new settlers, were fused together into one new culture, the culture of bronze. A deterioration in climate, coupled with improved skills and time acquired from new tools and weapons, brought about the creation of stone huts and enclosed fields that form small villages, littered across the face of the moor. A pattern of living developed that went on, fairly unchanged, into Roman times. All the available land on Dartmoor was probably taken up and may have spilled over into the valleys. Of all the moorland slopes in the Teign Valley, only Meldon shows no signs of hut circles or their remains, although there is some suggestion of lynchets, or terraces, on the steep side of the north-east.

The huts were built of solid granite blocks, sometimes double thickness, with thatched roofs of turf, reed or heather over a timber frame. Around them clustered the small enclosures where the cattle and sheep were brought for safe keeping. There are often remains of larger walled fields, where the grain was sown and harvested. The huts were generally built near a spring or close to a good supply of water.

New tools were invented, so that both hunting and farming could improve, and trade with the rest of Europe in tin brought finer workmanship from elsewhere. A Bronze Age palstave of Spanish type was found near Chagford.

Around 500 B.C. the deteriorating climate caused the marsh of the Somerset levels to be completely submerged, so that the only way of crossing this area was by timber trackway and the Polden Ridge. Glastonbury Tor remained an everlasting landmark for travellers in this area.

About 400 years before Christ a new wave of people arrived, and the Iron Age intruded into Devon. The newcomers spoke a Celtic language and together with the Bronze Age natives came to be a tribe known to the Romans as the Dumnonii. The use of a superior knowledge of metal-working gave these people domination over the native population, their language prevailed, and a growing population became more unified under chieftains. A warrior class, including women, emerged.

Forts, or rather defended dwelling places on high ground, date from this time; for example, the twin sites of Prestonbury and Cranbrook Castles, controlling the Teign Gorge. At Kestor, the Round Pound shows evidence of iron working, and this looks like a native Bronze Age settlement, which acquired the new skill and incorporated it into its own lifestyle. This was probably typical of the Dartmoor area, where a long-established pattern of living was not radically altered by the arrival of new people and new skills. It seems that the incoming people established an overlord-ship of the Bronze Age natives, who picked up their skills without being forced to move their habitat or alter their style of farming and living.

Around 100 B.C. a last wave of Celtic-speaking people arrived in southern England, this time fleeing from the Romans, whose imperialistic operations had now reached northern Europe. By the middle of the 1st century B.C. the Durotriges, a large tribe to the east of the Dumnonii, were minting coins, but there is no evidence of Dumnonian coins from this period, for in the south-west change comes slowly, and the destruction of the Celtic trading fleet by the Romans at that time made the south-west more cut off than before.

Slowly, but inevitably, the decision was reached; the Romans were to conquer Britain. In 55 B.C. and in 54 B.C. Caesar came to England, but not until A.D. 42 did the expedition of Claudius subdue the tribes of south-east England. Then began the task of subduing the tribes of the west and north.

Despite the warrior instincts of the Celtic people, their acknowledged courage, their artistic spirits, and their devotion to a religion which demanded a long and arduous training, they were no match for Roman legions.

By A.D. 47–48 the Dumnonii had recognised Rome as their master This can hardly have affected the lives of the Dartmoor people dramatically. A rural people, living in thatched huts, in banked or walled enclosures, on open moorland, were of no particular significance to the Romans, where they offered no resistance to Roman domination. The country was required to pay taxes to their new masters, which were collected at North Tawton. Precious metals were nationalised under the Romans, yet there is no evidence that they knew of the existence of tin or other metals on Dartmoor, and as a result probably left the natives undisturbed to continue their farming. Yet the native metalwork, both decorative and functional, continued to develop, and perhaps they found enough in the streams and hillsides for their own personal use, without the Romans ever becoming aware of it.

Roman civilisation crept nearer with time. Iron Age life had nothing resembling a town, and its closest approximation to roads were its ancient trackways, but the Romans created towns and built roads and down the roads came Roman legions, executives, and tax collectors. Exeter was founded, and a legion encamped there, while the road was continued towards Cornwall and probably reached at least as far as North Tawton.

The only Roman remains discovered in the Chagford area are some Roman coins found at Rushford, but how they came to be there is unknown.

Of other Roman remains there is no evidence. Although Exeter developed as a city during the Roman occupation, there are no signs of any Roman building west of that place. Christianity in some form reached as far as Roman Exeter, as sherds of pottery bearing Christian symbols prove, but it can hardly have penetrated the native population.

In the early 5th century Gaul was taken from the Romans, the Roman garrisons in Britain were cut off, and finally Rome withdrew. Some Latin had been absorbed into the native Celtic, coinage had appeared, new buildings and living styles had penetrated as far as Exeter, and then, suddenly, the Romans were gone. Some

200 years were to elapse before Saxon invaders arrived in the south-west, but, for a brief time, as Britain slipped into the Dark Ages, the south-west was given pause for breath.

It was during this pause that the first stirrings of Christianity appeared. Celtic pilgrims, travelling from Wales, Brittany and Ireland, slowly made their way to the rocky coasts of Devon and Cornwall, and the news of a new ideal, a new vision and a new religion came among the people of the south-west.

Although the pagan religion survived for some time, Christianity was overtaking it. For a people who had lost much of their original freedom, vitality and direction, without being absorbed into the more rarefied air of Roman life, it must have been an almost instinctive change of values and beliefs that they could embrace from people like themselves.

Chapter Two

THE KINGDOM OF DUMNONIA AND THE CREATION OF THE MANORS

PERHAPS THE CELTIC communities of the Chagford hillsides considered the withdrawal of the Romans a liberation. The primarily agricultural life style of the native people continued and developed. The south-west reverted to its tribal organisation. Dumnonia was once again a kingdom.

Little is definitely known about the events of those years. The tribal kingdoms of Britain developed their legends and fables, while a gradual introduction of Celtic Christianity re-shaped their ideals. This was the age of King Arthur of glorious memory, who may possibly have been from the Royal House of Dumnonia. One writer suggested that King's Oven may have been Arthur's Oven, and that his royal chair was situated on Dartmoor.

The south-west had close connections with Wales and was known for some time as West Wales, hence the name Walla Brook, meaning Welshman's Brook. The North Walla Brook running from King's Oven records a Celtic settlement there, in its name.

The pagan religion of the Celts was known to the Romans and later to the Saxons as the Druidic religion and Druid's Well at Middlecott suggests that, at least by the coming of the Saxons, the native population had begun to cultivate the valleys.

The Celtic people were particularly skilled at metalwork and made ornamental objects with decorative patterns in their characteristic circular style. Despite their tradition of being fearless warriors, they seem to have absorbed Christianity in a manner equally as passionate. Christianity arrived from both west and east. From the west, Celtic missionaries settled in remote spots, often on the coast or in dense forest, in imitation of Christ's solitary vigil in the wilderness. They built small huts or cells and practised a form of dedicated and rigorous self-denial, in order to follow the teaching of Christ.

We know that they arrived around the coast of Devon and Cornwall quite extensively in the period 490-690, and some early churches were dedicated to these saintly founders. Perhaps they never came as far inland as Chagford, but their influence in the kingdom had certainly arrived.

From the east, Christianity spread through the vehicle of the Roman Empire, which provided a natural means for the spread of new ideas throughout most of Europe. During the occupation of Britain there were some conversions to Christianity, but when the Roman Empire adopted the new religion that it had previously persecuted, so missionaries came from Rome to convert the heathen. Saxon occupation of Britain occurred at a time when Rome was sending such missionaries to the Saxon kings.

The earliest Christianity on Dartmoor was almost certainly Celtic in origin, but it was closely followed by Christianity from Rome, adopted by the Saxons.

The last possible influence for early Christianity must be Glastonbury. The legends and myths, the extraordinary religious significance of the place must be built around some original truth. Glastonbury had been a centre of settlement in earlier times, was a landmark for travellers to and from the south-west, and, as a natural outcrop in a flat wilderness, it is distinct from far away. It seems natural that early Celtic missionaries, arriving on the coast, should choose to settle there. Whoever brought Christianity to Glastonbury, it is certainly one of Britain's earliest foundations.

One of the earliest evangelists of Christianity was born in Crediton in 680. Although the Saxons had not finally subdued Dumnonia at this time, some already were settled in the south-west, for the parents of Winfrith, later to become St. Boniface, were Anglo-Saxon. Winfrith was educated at a religious house in Exeter and later near Southampton. He became the great evangelist of Germany, and died a martyr in Frisia in 755. Crediton, the birthplace of St. Boniface, became the site of a monastery in 739, and it would be strange if the influence of this Christian community had not spread the 12 miles to Chagford.

Whether an early church stood where Chagford church now stands, or even before that the spot was a pagan shrine, only extensive excavation could show. The form of the graveyard, raised and walled, is similar to a type that existed from the 5th until the 9th century, or even later. The stone crosses that once stood in the Square might have served as standing stones and perhaps the cross tree, that until recently stood outside the church gates, might have been a descendant of an earlier sacred grove.

Chagford church, like Glastonbury Tower and St. Michael's Mount, is dedicated to St. Michael the Archangel. It has been suggested that there is a line of churches dedicated to St. Michael running from Bury St. Edmunds to St. Michael's Mount, and this would include Chagford. Whether the early Christians employed such methods remains conjecture.

Chagford church was dedicated by Bishop Branescombe in 1261, but this must be much later than its foundation. A wooden chapel may have been the first Christian church, and only later was a stone church built to replace it.

As the new religion spread among the Celtic tribes, a new race of people began to infiltrate the area. The Saxons probably arrived in small groups of settlers in the 6th century, and may have been tolerated by the native people until their numbers and influence began to grow. The first battle against the Saxons in the south-west occurred in 614, but it was not until the following century that Devon became part of the Saxon kingdom of Wessex. Christianity now came under the influence of the Roman-inspired Christianity of south-eastern England, and Devon was part of the see of Sherborne until 909, when the dioceses of Crediton, Wells and St. Germans were founded.

Chagford is a Saxon name, originally spelt Kagefort, and meaning Gorse Ford—Chagford being the Gorsey spot, where the River Teign was forded. Few Celtic names survive in Devon, the Saxons quickly infiltrating and conquering the kingdom, so that their names remain. Many of the native people fled to Brittany with the coming of the Saxons, but where pockets of them were left on the hillsides, the Saxons would tend to record that fact in the way that they named the place, as in the Walla Brook.

The Saxons had a tradition of forest dwelling, and it is most likely that they, rather than the Celts, cleared the forest in the Teign Valley ready for agriculture. Their language and their lifestyle took over. The creation of farms and vills, the system of land-holding under feudal lords later flowered into the full feudal stystem of the Normans. It is unlikely that many of the Celtic people could remain free on their own terms. The names of the landowners in 1066 are consistently Saxon. The Celtic people on Dartmoor seem to have melted away as the land passed into the hands of a new race. Saxon land-holding shows only the faint beginning of the feudal system. Some land was held by traditional right, some was given in freehold, and later some was leased for limited periods in return for services rendered to an overlord.

The 8th and 9th centuries were the time when Chagford was absorbed into Wessex, soon to be overlord of the Kingdom of England. The hundreds, the earliest division of land for administrative purposes, were set out, and the hundred of Wonford, in which Chagford stood, was created among them.

Saxon buildings were generally of wood, with the result that little trace of them is left today. They left their mark only through the creation of their ploughlands and their contribution to the early Norman feudal system.

Neither do we know which gods Dodo, Alric, Edwi, and Alwin served, or even where these men lived. Dodo, for example, was the possessor of 10 manors recorded in the Devonshire Domesday, and may have had his home nowhere near Chagford. Who his ceorls, geneats, geburs, cotsetles and theows, or in other words his work force were, again goes unrecorded.

What we do have from early days, though their age cannot be fixed, are the granite crosses which stand beside so many Devon roads and in some of the wildest places. Tradition says that a cross once stood at 'Watching Place', marking the spot where the moorland Christian British awaited the onslaught of the Saxon invaders, and where they fought their battle. The cross was known as Beetor Cross, and was taken down by a landowner, some hundred years ago, to be used as a gatepost. It is quite plain and now stands in the hedge at the placed named after it, where the road turns away towards Manaton.

Another simple granite cross stands on Week Down which, among the crosses of the parish, has moved the shortest distance in recorded history. In 1867 a bank gave way and the cross had to be shifted slightly from its original site. It was leaning before it was moved, and so it was re-erected in the same manner. A Maltese cross has been incised on both sides, between the arms, but when this was done is unknown.

A cross once stood on the north side of the market place in Chagford, but this one suffered a cruel fate. Its base was removed to Southmead House, by a Mr. Southmead, then lord of the manor, while he moved the cross itself to Holy Street Manor, where it lay for many years in the farmyard. Later the Rev. A. Whipham, in an attempt to preserve it, had it built into a wall at Holy Street.

A second cross stood on the south side of the market place, but this, too, was removed and taken to Waye Barton by Mr. Coniam, where it was used as a gate post. It was obviously damaged in its life there; when Ormerod, the Victorian antiquarian, found it, it was lying in a rubbish heap at the back of the barn. It has a Latin cross incised between its arms and has now been re-erected on the common behind Waye Barton.

Ormerod says a cross known as Stumpy Cross stood a little way from the village, on the Okehampton road, by the entrance to South Huish, but already by his time there was no trace of it.

Short Cross stands between Week Down and Middlecott and is said to occupy its original site, despite being removed by Mr. Clampitt of Middlecott, in Victorian times, to be put under the pump in his farmyard.

Four small crosses were removed from the pinnacles of the church tower, during restoration work, and one further cross was used as a gatepost at Teigncombe.

Some of these crosses may date back to the earliest introduction of Christianity into the area, some might have once been standing stones, cut into crosses as Christianity began to take the place of the previous religion. The incised crosses that some bear may have been cut at a later date, to mark differing schools of the early church. These are the only vague hints of the coming of a religion that later would be the key to village life.

Chagford's ancient wealth was not only its farming land, but its minerals. The use of tin had begun in prehistoric times in the south-west, and although there is no evidence that tin was mined on Dartmoor, as it was in Cornwall during the Bronze and Iron Ages, it seems likely that the prosperous Bronze Age communities of the Teign Valley would have found enough of the precious metal in the bed of the river, or under the peat, to supply their own needs.

Coins of tin were minted at Lydford in Saxon times; later Burghs gained this privilege, and Exeter had the right to a mint. Lydford was the centre of the mining industry and the second oldest town in Devon, presumably reflecting the importance of precious metals. The Teign valley was rich in ore and the Saxons are unlikely to have been completely unaware of this.

As if the changes of the previous 300 years had not been sufficient, the 11th century brought the arrival of the Danes. In 997 they sailed up the Tamar, but were beaten back by the tinners at Lydford, but it was not long before they gained control of the English Channel.

In 1017 Cnut became the first Danish king of England; and Chagford, like all England, was required to pay its danegeld for the upkeep of the king.

The Danes and the Saxons were close enough in temperament and lifestyle to co-exist, but only 50 years elapsed before William of Normandy crossed the Channel and England became the possession of the Norman kings.

It was the farming communities created by the Saxons and Danes which the Domesday Commissioners recorded in 1086. By then there were five such holdings within our parish boundaries, all part of the hundred of Wonford, whose mote-stowe, or administrative centre, was at Exe-bridge. The owners of these early farms were people called Dodo, Alric, Edwi and Alwin. Their holdings amounted to something like 360 acres of arable land for which they paid geld.

The Domesday Book records five manors in the Chagford parish, two of which border on the moor. Yet by that time there was little left of those busy moorland villages that had survived the Roman invasion. Moorland agriculture, Celtic tribal life, and the religions of those early people had disappeared from the gentle slopes of the Teign valley. They had been replaced by the manors of Chageford, Taincombe, Shapley, Risford, Midelcote, and South Taine.

Chapter Three

MEDIEVAL CHAGFORD

WHEN THE DOMESDAY BOOK was compiled in 1086 Chagford was hardly a village as we understand the word. The parish consisted of several agricultural communities settled amid large tracts of virgin forest. The moorland had only sparse tree cover, but it was no longer occupied as it had once been.

The Saxon settlements supported a tiny population who now became the working parts in the complex machinery of the Norman feudal kingdom. This is true, too of any Celtic or even Romano-British people who had held their land through the Saxon invasions and who, by now, must have become an integral part of Saxon rural life.

With the coming of the Norman kings the system of land ownership and use went through a change which was both subtle and fundamental. Land was no longer owned outright, but was the property of the crown, held from the king in return for allegiance and military service. The king parcelled out his newly-conquered island to his greater nobles and churchmen. They were required to provide a force of so many men in return. To do this they settled knights on their several manors who would provide the necessary military service for the king. The farming men, who worked the land and were inherited with it as though they were a barn or a cowshed, were in a similar role of obligation, but their service was agricultural work on the lord of the manor's land in return for the use of their own private acres. Along with Norman knights who became lords of English manors, some Saxon thanes were re-allotted their lands by the king in return for their feudal allegiance.

In addition the classes of working men were regulated by divisions of status, which gave them their rights, duties and freedoms.

A villein had the right to work a piece of land which might be as big as 30 acres, and had rights of pasture and meadow, but he must contribute his oxen to the village plough team, and do his regulation number of days on the manorial land. He might have other duties allotted to him, and, later, fines and restrictions were imposed which limited his right to marry off his daughters or pass his land on to his sons.

Serfs were no better than slaves, but disappeared as a class soon after the Norman invasion.

Bordars or cottars were cottagers, with a few acres of land, who earned their living as labourers, supplemented by whatever they could grow.

The freemen, of whom a surprising number seem to have survived in this area, rented their land from the lord of the manor, but owed him no other obligation. These were the people who carved out the early farms in the more remote parts of the parish and who became the yeomen and gentry of later years.

The five manors in the parish, mentioned in the Domesday Book, suffered different fates. The manor of Chagford and the manor of Teigncombe were given into the hands of the Bishop of Coutances, and held from him by a man named Drogo, whose name must make him a Saxon thane.

Rushford became the property of Baldwin, Sheriff of Devon, and was held by Edwi, who had held it in the time of Edward the Confessor. Midelcote remained in the hands of Alwin.

Shapley went to Baldwin and was held by a man named Godwin. So, although the overlordship altered, the lords of the manors were, in 1086, still Saxon thanes.

The Domesday Book says of the Manor of Chageford, or Kagefort, as it was variously spelled:

> Chageford was held by Dodo in the time of King Edward, and paid geld for one hide. There is land for six ploughs. in demesne is one plough, and there are four serfs, and eight villeins, and five bordars, with one plough and a half. There are eighteen acres of meadow, and sixty acres of pasture, and fifteen acres of wood. Formerly worth twenty shillings, it is now worth thirty shillings.

There are all kinds of problems with translating this information into our own language. Firstly the Domesday Book was written in a matter of months, by a few clerks who would be sent into an area to elicit the necessary information from the natives. Difficulties with language and dialect, along with inconsistencies in units of measurement, would have created enough problems. In addition the country had been conquered only 20 years before and had gone through intense upheavals and convulsions. Isolated districts probably went in some fear of the new rulers, and it is not hard to imagine if tax collectors rode into a tiny moorland hamlet, speaking French, just how accurate their record would be. The natives could have told them anything that was not contradicted at first glance.

But even assuming the Domesday Book is fairly accurate, units of measurement have changed so much and were in any case not the same throughout the country that even so careful a record as the Domesday Book gives an uncertain picture of the size of the manorial lands.

The quantities are given in number of ploughs. One plough was generally pulled by eight oxen and the amount of land means the amount that such a team could plough in one year. One plough is roughly one hide, which is roughly 100 acres.

The demesne is the lord's own land, worked for him by his villeins, who owned cattle enough to make up a second and third plough team.

The fact that the cattle were on hand to be harnessed up is no guarantee that they were used to their fullest extent, while the infield–outfield system, which allotted the various parcels of land, gave a system of some shifting cultivation. Only the infield was continuously cultivated; the outfield was cultivated piece by piece, and in rotation, returning after several years to rough grazing, as a new part was cultivated.

The infield was the site of the characteristic strips of land held by the several villeins. The entire infield of the manor or village was divided into either two or three portions. One would be left fallow, while the other(s) were ploughed, and rotation of the fallow area kept the soil fertile. Each of these portions was then

TABLE I. DOMESDAY MANORS

Exeter Book	Exchequer Book	Held by	OverLord	Demesne	Total Land	Work Force + Their Land	Meadow	Pasture	Wood	Animals
KAGEFORT	Chageford	Dodo before 1066	Bishop of COUTANCES	1 Plough	6 Ploughs	4 Serfs, 8 Villeins 5 Bordars 1½ Ploughs	18 Acres	60 Acres	15 Acres	5 Cattle 41 Sheep
TAINCOMA	Taincome	Alric before 1066 Drogo after 1066	Bishop of COUTANCES Bishop of COUTANCES	1 Plough 1½ Ferling	4 Ploughs	2 Serfs, 6 Villeins 2 Bordars 1½ Ploughs	4 Acres	3 Leugas x 1 Leuga	4 Acres	6 Cattle 5 Swine 20 Sheep 14 Goats
RISFORT	Risford	Edwi before and after 1066	Baldwin SHERIFF of Devon	1 Plough 1½ Virgates	5 Ploughs	1 Serf, 8 Villeins 5 Bordars 3 Ploughs 2½ Virgates	5 Acres	4 Acres	4 Acres COPPICE	9 Cattle 59 Sheep
MIDELCOTA	Midelcote	Alwin before and after 1066	Alwin	1 Plough	1 Plough	1 Serf			3 Acres COPPICE	4 Cattle 34 Sheep 10 Goats
ESCAPELEIA	Scapelie	Uluric before 1066 Godwin after 1066	Baldwin Baldwin	½ Virgate	3 Ploughs	1 Serf, 4 Villeins 1½ Ploughs ½ Virgate	5 Acres			

divided into furlong strips and each villein would work his strip beside his fellows. The interdependence of the plough teams, and the system of many men working strips of one large field, had everyone growing the same crop and following the same schedule.

Table I records the various states of the Chagford manors. Only one was held directly from the king—Midelcote, and that was small and lacking men. Chagford manor was grazing a considerable number of sheep, perhaps on the slopes of Meldon.

Teigncombe shows the largest range of animals, with both swine and goats; poultry is not mentioned, although it was almost certainly kept, nor is honey, although bees had been domesticated by this time in some parts of England. It is hard to guess just how much land was being ploughed and sown, year by year, in the parish. If one plough was really 100 acres, the 17 men who worked the Chagford manor would have been ploughing, sowing and reaping on 600 acres, apart from tending sheep, milking cows, thatching and repairing their dwellings and barns, keeping their harness and implements in good trim, and getting the quantities of wood that were needed, not only for warmth, but for cooking. Poultry had to be cared for, vegetables grown, clothes, and sometimes shoes, had to be provided.

The Domesday Book makes no mention of women or children, and where the work-force seems insufficient for the size of the holding, it may well be that much of the work was being done by the womenfolk and young children.

None of the buildings of the early Norman period have survived, with the result that we do not know where these various manors had their boundaries, dwellings or focus. A manor need not have a manor house, if its lord lived elsewhere. There would be the barns, the cattle shed and the cottages of the villeins and cottagers. The hall of the lord of the manor might be set away from these buildings, near its own demesne.

The manor of Rushford must have occupied what is now Rushford Mill and Rushford Barton, with Lower and Higher Withecombe and Rushford Wood. There was probably a manor here, perhaps a little forward of the present Rushford Barton, for the later owners seem to have lived there throughout medieval times.

Teigncombe Manor was between Meldon, Kestor and the Teign, and must have had its centre roughly where the present farm of Teigncombe is. Later it seems to have devolved into the manor of Collerewe.

The manor of Chagford is a little more difficult to locate. The manorial farm grew into a hamlet and then a village in a comparatively short time, and the cottages and farm buildings of the original manor probably stood where the village stands today. The manorial lands must have stretched from Padley Common down the banks of the river, perhaps almost as far as Easton and bordering on Great Week. Orchard Cottage is probably roughly the site of the manorial farm and the field below is likely enough the main infield of the villeins. The demesne was probably situated higher up near Waye Barton.

One other manor crossed the present borders of the parish and that was the manor of South Teign. It was a royal manor from early times and included Easton and Great Week, while the remainder of its land was in the parish of Moretonhampstead.

The siting of the Chagford manor led it to become the focus for the other manors, so that it grew into a proper village, with the village church at its centre, and a market to increase prosperity.

The boundary of each manor may not have been sharply defined, but over the next two centuries the creation of small, semi-independent farms created the land pattern we know today. Freemen gained charters from the lord of the manor to clear the forest at the edges of the manorial area and to create farms for themselves, for which they paid a small rent. In clearing the land of the boulders, that many eras before severe frost and mighty rivers had strewn over its surface, they built walls and lanes that stand unchanged into our own times. The lanes grew naturally as one small farm made a track between its high-walled fields to the next farm down the valley, and they were necessarily small, twisting and unplanned.

At this time the whole of Devon was legally the King's Forest, which limited the people's right to hunt and pasture their animals. In 1204 the people of Devon paid 5,000 marks for the disafforestation of the county, apart from the moor itself, which remained the King's Forest of Dartmoor. Thereafter the bordering parishes paid a Venville rent for the privilege of pasturing their animals on the moor.

The Devonshire longhouse, or long farmhouse, with its characteristic central passage and long chambers either side—one for cattle and one for people—is a style that lasted for centuries, and it would be difficult to date the many fine granite farmhouses that are found all over the parish. The names are some reference to their earliest foundation.

Names ending in Worthy, meaning an enclosed homestead, are Saxon in origin and probably indicate farmsteads first settled in Saxon times. For example, Batworthy, earlier Badworthy, Yardworthy, Thornworthy, and Fernworthy are all early settlements. Alternatively, these could be the remnants of Celtic farmsteads surviving among and named by the incoming Saxons. The fact that the names are old only shows that settlements occurred at these places from early times. There is no indication that any farmhouses date from the Saxon or early Norman period. A fine granite porch at Yardworthy, although the house it belonged to no longer stands, has been tentatively dated as 14th-century, and must be the oldest remnant of the Norman farmhouses of the parish.

As for the early names, Jurston means Jordan's farm, presumably from its original inhabitant. Drewston is derived from Thurwardeston, and there was a Thorward in the parish in 1333, whose family probably settled it. Holy Street was called Hall-Start in 1219, but was 11th-century in origin. Stiniel was Stone Hall in 1224, North and South Hill was the home of John le Hull in 1249, Hole was the property of William atte Hole, and Thorn belonged to Robert atte Thorn in 1333. Venn was the home of Stephen de la Fenne, while Yeo belonged to Walter atte Yo, meaning Walter at the water. These names, which are a mixture of Saxon and Norman, are probably the names of some of the early freemen who settled the smaller farms, independent of, but still subordinate to, the principal manors.

In the world outside, changes were slowly coming. In 1100 there were only four towns in Devon: Exeter, Lydford, Totnes, and Barnstaple. Between 1066 and 1086 Baldwin, Sheriff of Devon and Baron of Okehampton, had built the castle of

Fig. 2. Teign Head Farm, Chagford (from an etching by Samuel Prout)

Okehampton and had a market there. This was the beginning of what was to be the borough. Here Baldwin lived and administered his many properties. The road had stretched west from Exeter in Roman times, perhaps before, and now linked the splendid medieval city of Exeter with the isolated fortress of Okehampton. Few people from Chagford can have had time or means to travel so far in either direction.

Chagford stood on the King's Way, a trackway of indefinite age, which crossed the moor from Exeter. From Exeter the route passed to Dunsford and crossed the Teign at Clifford Bridge, went past Cranbrook and Uppacott to Easton, and after passing through Chagford, continued up Waye Hill, following the lane to Thorn and Metherall and then crossed Hurston Ridge to join the now modern road at the western foot of Merripit Hill.

Bridges were few, although Chagford Bridge was in existence in 1224 and must have led up to Gidleigh and Throwleigh, two settlements intimately connected with Chagford in medieval times.

At about this time there were already cloth mills at Chagford Bridge, owned by a family named de Ponte. An old deed between Hugh de Chagford and one of the de Ponte family refers to a piece of demesne land, near the old burial ground in Chagford, but I cannot trace it more closely.

The original Holy Street mill was 11th century in origin and ground corn. It may well have been the mill for the manor of Teigncombe. Rushford mill was the original mill for the Manor of Rushford. The stepping-stones beside it probably pre-date Rushford Bridge as a means of crossing the River Teign from the Manor of Rushford to reach Chagford. Sandy Park mill (now the *Mill End* hotel) probably served Easton, while Batworthy mill must have ground corn for the moorland areas of the parish. All of these mills, with the exception of Batworthy, used water from the Teign, Batworthy used the River Bovey.

With regard to law and order, village matters were settled at the manorial court by the lord of the manor. Other crimes or legal disputes went to the Hundred Court of Exebridge, or to the Shire Courts, where the village was represented by the reeve (or village foreman), the priest, and 'four better men'.

Many village churches were built by the lord of the manor, which, aside from religious motives, would give his manor an added focus and prestige. Chagford church was dedicated by Bishop Bronescombe, Bishop of Exeter, in 1261, when the de Chagfords were lords of the manor. It was perhaps Henry de Chagford who was responsible for the building of the church and who then held the patronage of the living, or the right to appoint the clergymen. The earliest clergyman whose name we know is Simon de Wibbery, who was rector of Chagford in 1315.

The de Chagfords, in the person of Thomas de Chagford, are recorded as having sold the manor and advowson of Chagford to this Simon de Wibbery in 1299, but, in fact, the two families were already inter-married, and if there was an exchange of money it may have been more in the nature of a consideration so that Simon, rather than another member of the family, should gain the manor and advowson.

The upkeep of the rector was provided for by glebe land and by tithes. Glebe land was generally provided by the lord of the manor when he built the church, and the rector himself would have to cultivate it, besides fulfilling his religious duties. Although this made him as dependent on weather and the seasons as his flock, he must have had to work hard. The tithing system had been established in early Christian times, from the words of Christ himself, who had called for charity to the poor and needy. The church came to fix a standard rate for the payment of tithes, which in some cases were used solely for the upkeep of the rector and in other cases for many good causes within the parish. Every member of the community was required to give one-tenth of his yearly produce, and the times for the giving of them were regulated by the church calendar. The tithings were brought to the church porch on the feast of St. Michael.

It was only churches and chapels with burial grounds which were entitled to tithes, and this must be the principal difference between Chagford church and the several manorial chapels in the parish. If the village church was far from the outlying manors and difficult to get to in bad weather, the lords of the manors could apply to the bishop to build a chapel on their own manor and celebrate divine service there. There were three such chapels in the parish: at Teigncombe, Rushford and Great Week. Sadly none of these have survived.

Village life centred around the church, which was the central organisation of the parish. The church guilds, of which there were at one time 13 in Chagford, were responsible for the many duties applicable to the church itself—its linen, its candles, its proper care and maintenance, but they also organised feasts, and brewed ale.

A riotous evening with a good quantity of ale was a principal form of entertainment in those days, and was known as scotale. So, if one were to see one's neighbour tottering along the lanes late at night in a ferocious frame of mind, and it seems that ale was very potent in those days, you'd know he'd been on a scotale.

The Norman knights who arrived with the Conqueror provide the names of the earliest great families of the parish. The ancient family of Prouz, whose home was Gidleigh Castle, were great land-owners in the area, and though they never owned the Manor of Chagford itself, they were related to the lords of Chagford Manor and later came to live at Waye.

The family of Wibbery held the Chagford manor and advowson from 1299, and provided the first two rectors of Chagford whose names we know. The Wibbery family descended through several generations to a certain John Wibbery, who married a lady named Leva Gorges. The family of Gorges had come from a village of that name north of Coutances in Normandy, and Ralph de Gorges had fought at Hastings. When the Norman kings lost their French dukedom the last of the family had come to England. They had acquired lands in Devon and it was the heiress of this family that John Wibbery married. Their daughter, Joan, married John Bonville of Shute, whose father was to become the second husband of Leva Gorges. Their daughter, Anna, thus became the heiress of Gorges, Wibbery and Bonville. Anna owned among her possessions the Manor of Chagford and this then passed at her marriage to her husband, Philip Coplestone.

Rushford Manor was in the hands of the de Risfords until the reign of Richard II, when the heiress of the family married a man named Hoare, into whose family it then passed. They were then the owners of the property until the 18th century.

The principal difficulty with the feudal system is that land was held, as it were, through a chain of command, whose author was the king, but which may have many connected links. For example, the Manor of Rushford is recorded on the one hand as having belonged directly to the de Risfords, followed by the Hoares, but on the other hand it is also recorded as having been held by the following people: in 1285 by Nicholas Crespyn; in 1303 by Robert de Forde; in 1346 by Robert de Forde, afterwards by John Berkedon; and in 1428 by William Monk of Potheridge and four other freeholders.

If a family gave up holding a manor, they might retain some of the rights belonging to it; alternatively, if they held several manors, they might choose to settle a freeholder, or knight, on one or more of them, in which case the actual tenant would hold that manor of the original family, who might hold it from a baron, who might hold it from the king. This is probably what happened to Rushford.

Midelcote, along with Great Week, came to be part of a manor called South Teign, which was the property of Edmund, Earl of Cornwall, in 1301, and later was a royal manor held by the Duke of Cornwall, who was also the Prince of Wales and eldest son of the king.

Teigncombe came into the hands of Simon de Wibbery in 1303 and from them on the manors of Teigncombe and Chagford seem to have been held jointly at least until Tudor times.

The manors of the Hundred were grouped into townships in 1316, because the Lincoln parliament of that year had called upon each township 'to furnish the King with one man at arms'. Among the listings for the Hundred of Wonford is given: 'Township of Throwleigh with Chagford, Shilston and Spreyton its members, of which Roger de Moelys is lord.' This Roger de Moelys married Alice Prouz of Gidleigh and Throwleigh, and their daughter, Isolda, married into the family of Wibbery and de Chagford. At this time the manors of Gidleigh, Throwleigh and Chagford were all in one family.

Chagford's prosperity grew out of its market. Once a market had been granted to the lord of the manor, the increase in revenue that arose from more trade and the tolls paid by stall-holders, the manor or village was destined to become a more prosperous place.

In 1219-20, Hugh de Chagford was summoned to the King's Court to show by what warrant he had set up a market at Chagford, to the injury of the market of Earl William de Mandeville in Moreton, without the King's licence. 'Hugh says he has not so set up a market, because his market was set up a hundred years ago, and the Earl's market was set up five years ago, and both were on Sunday until they were changed to Saturday out of regard to religion.

'The Earl, by his attorney, says that Hugh never had a market at Chagford, save that a certain assembly sometimes came together on Sunday at which meat and bread and so forth were sold. Afterwards his father, Geoffrey Fitz Peter, came and spoke with King John so that the King granted him his market at Moreton, where formerly there used to be an assembly as at Chagford, and then the King prohibited the market and assembly of Chagford, but only through the war and force of war.

'Hugh says that no such prohibition was ever made to him, and that he takes toll and stallage in his market such as ought to be taken in a market, and has always taken it.

'The Earl denying that toll was taken there before the war, orders are given to summon a jury of men of Chagford and of Moreton to inquire "if there was a market at Chagford receiving toll, stallage and other customs which pertain to a market before King John granted a market to Geoffrey Fitz Piers, Earl of Essex".'

King John had died in 1216; Henry III was on the throne, and the reign of the robber barons was coming to an end. It seems probable that this dispute was settled in favour of Chagford, since Moreton was granted a charter for a market again in 1335. Polewhele, writing in the 18th century states that Chagford's charter was lost in a fire that destroyed the town at the close of the 17th century. However, in 1574 the documents were in the custody of the 'four men', who were senior churchwardens. The market remained the possession of the lord of the manor until the 16th century.

Apart from the village markets, towns or boroughs might hold fairs to attract trade from far away, even foreign merchants, along with travelling players, wandering friars, and an assortment of goods never seen during the course of the year. Such a fair was held in Exeter and must have provided tremendous excitement and entertainment to those able to attend.

The Chagford market was no doubt held in the square, which might have been cobbled in medieval days, but equally could have remained as earth. None of the present houses date from the Middle Ages, with the exception of the Bishop's House, which tradition dates as 13th century, although there is no proof of its date. Nor does there appear to be any record of its original owner or occupant, apart from its tantalising name, which could be younger than the house ifself. Its present inhabitants have seen the ghost or spirit of a young woman, who seems to be dressed roughly in medieval costume, who was drawn forth by playing a mandolin in the garden on a summer's evening. It must have reminded her of the music of her own times, perhaps the dulcimer or lute, so she must have come from a time when such instruments were heard in Chagford and from among the sort of people who might play them. An ecclesiastical family of some kind would provide this background, but equally a prosperous merchant might have brought the instrument home for his precious daughter. This is all conjecture and the young lady is not likely to tell us.

The church is, of course, the earliest existing building in the village and deserves a chapter to itself. Such time, money and energy not only went into the original building, and the later additions, but religious changes and upheavals brought new fashions in church furniture and decoration, all of which had to be executed and paid for by the efforts of the community.

One other building, no longer extant, was fundamental to Chagford's prosperity. That was the Stannary Court, which stood in the square and was the place where the tin was weighed, taxed and had the king's stamp put on it. Tin had been extracted from the granite masses of the south-west since antiquity, but had apparently completely disappeared until the 12th century, when it was discovered in the slopes and streams of Dartmoor. Something like a tin rush must have occurred, with the tiny moorland parishes suddenly the possessors of a valuable mineral. Apparently the Blowing Houses, where the tin was smelted were once known as Jews' Houses, which could suggest that Jews were instrumental in the rise of the Dartmoor tin industry, although this could be a confusion of pronunciation, or even a term of abuse.

The tin industry grew quickly from the late 1100s, and the greatest prosperity was in these early years. In the following century the centre of the industry moved to Cornwall, but in the halcyon days from about 1160 to the early part of the next century, Devon was the tin centre of Europe. Four Dartmoor villages were given the distinction of being Stannary Towns, where the tin was weighed, stamped and where duty was paid on it: Ashburton, Tavistock, and Plympton, with Chagford, covered roughly the four quarters of the moor. Chagford was created a Stannary Town in 1305, but the industry had already brought some prosperity to the former village, and it is probable that the size and beauty of Chagford church owes some debt to the wealth arising from the previous mineral.

There are numerous sites of tin streaming all over the parish, and the later churchwarden's accounts make continual reference to the tinners. So much of the prosperity and importance of Chagford in medieval and Tudor times is bound up with tinning, that it, too, must have a separate chapter. Suffice it to say here that the Stannary Court brought merchants from distant places, the king's officers to stamp the tin and collect the duty, and the tinners themselves gained a new, if hard-earned, wealth, which contributed through tithes and through family prosperity to the wealth of the town.

The Crusades had been fought by English knights and soldiers since 1096, but it was the ships returning from the Near East that brought to England a plague that effectively destroyed the feudal system. In 1381 the Black Death arrived via the ports of Southampton and Bristol and was responsible for the death of something like a third of the population of England. Between 1377 and 1381 the population of Devon had been halved, and there is little doubt that the population of Chagford had suffered accordingly. Sheep were also hit by the plague, the tin industry suffered as a result of the shortage of labour, but more importantly there was a chronic shortage of agricultural workers. A law was passed prohibiting demands for increased wages and labourers leaving their manors, but the effect was only to cause intense discontent in the countryside, leading to the Peasant's Revolt.

Unrest had shown itself at Chagford in 1380, the year before the Black Death, when a certain Henry Fulford was accused with others of rioting in Chagford, attacking Thomas Creedy, sergeant-at-arms (an officer of the Crown), and hindering him and his servants in the arrest of certain malefactors. In 1382 an order was given 'to arrest all homicides, robbers and insurgents, now more than usually present in the counties of Somerset, Dorset, Devon and Cornwall, as well as their maintainers and notorious suspects and deliver them to the gaol of the county in which the offence is committed, as it appears they escape from one county to another'. Law and order had broken down. A century earlier, in 1285, Thomas de Chagford was recorded with the traditional lord of the manor's 'liberty to gallows, tumbrel, assize of bread and beer, waifs and strays, pleas of blood and claims of theft, as also view of frankpledge from time out of mind'. But with the shortage of labour and widespread unrest it seems that the traditional means of keeping the peace were no longer sufficient.

Order was restored to the countryside, and the tin industry went back into full prosperity, but the feudal system never recovered. Many work services had already been commuted into money rents, and this was the general rule throughout the remainder of the Middle Ages. Most men gained their freedom and became, if not the owners of their land, at least its free tenant.

The late Middle ages found John Bonville the owner of the manor of Chagford. His great-grandmother had been the daughter of Alice Prouz and Roger de Moelys. When Roger de Moelys died Alice was abducted by a certain John Daumarle, apparently because he was determined to marry her. Perhaps the arrangements had already been made, but he must have been in some concern about the properties he might inherit through his new bride, when he abducted her. The confusion of the legalities of inheritance is intense, for Alice had a son by John Daumarle who inherited the manor of Gidleigh, whereas Alice's daughter by Roger de Moelys married a de Chagford, who retained the manor of Chagford to pass to his son. This is typical of the way in which land was inherited under the feudal system, and of how the nobles increased their holdings by series of judicious marriages.

The family of Prouz was an ancient Norman family, connected by marriage to the Conqueror himself, and owned much land in Devon. In 1240 Sir William de Prouz was one of 12 knights who made a perambulation of the forest of Dartmoor, with the Sheriff of Devon to make notes of its exact bounds. The bounds they recorded differ little from those of today. One Peter de Prouz married the daughter of the Earl of Devon, and thereby acquired for his children one-third of all the earl's land in England. A Sir William Prouz married the daughter of Sir Fulk Ferrers, and then had the adjoining manor of Throwleigh. After Alice Prouz married and Chagford went to the Bonvilles, and Gidleigh via the Daumarles to the Coades, the principal members of the family were centred on their other lands. However, many of them married into Chagford families and later came to live at Waye, holding Shapley manor from 1292–1639.

Their coat-of-arms is on a shield in Chagford church and not far from it, suspended on high, is a small model of an esquire's helmet of the kind that was once borne in funeral pageants.

One further note about the early Prouz family. In 1294 Hugh le Pruz was among 25 Devon knights summoned to proceed to Wales and suppress a rising under a Welsh chieftain named Madog. In 1324 he had become one of the six knights 'incapable of exertion', but liable for military service against the Scots. Such was the business of a knight.

Chagford was not without its royal connections. In 1204 King John fixed by charter the dowry of his Queen Isabella, which included Easton and Great Week in Chagford, in fact, the part of Chagford which was the royal manor of South Teign. Only 11 years later King John granted to Richard Malherbe the land of Great Week, Easton and Slaucombe, later written Thorncumb, which is Thorn in Easton. The most obvious conclusion is that John had just granted away part of his wife's dowry.

While these great and military men gained and lost their various manors, freemen were prospering on their own farms, while villeins also gained their freedom and began to enjoy a greater prosperity of their own. The horse began to take over as a plough animal, and the quality of domestic animals had inproved. Life on the Chagford farm was not so far from the kind of life that disappeared with the emergence of the tractor. In 1480 the Churchwarden's Accounts begin, and from then on there is a far more intimate picture of the workings of the community.

PROUZ of GIDLEIGH and CHAGFORD
1100-1600 (approx.)

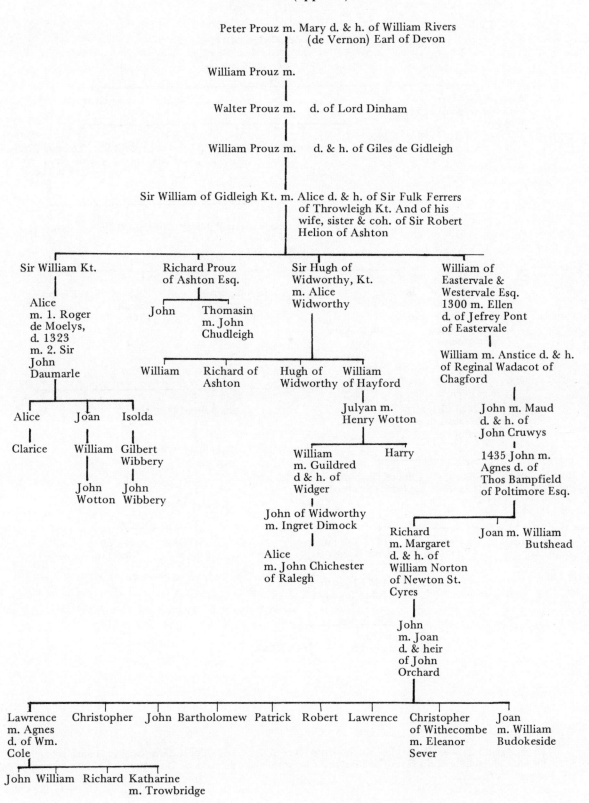

Peter Prouz m. Mary d. & h. of William Rivers
(de Vernon) Earl of Devon

William Prouz m.

Walter Prouz m.   d. of Lord Dinham

William Prouz m.   d. & h. of Giles de Gidleigh

Sir William of Gidleigh Kt. m. Alice d. & h. of Sir Fulk Ferrers
of Throwleigh Kt. And of his
wife, sister & coh. of Sir Robert
Helion of Ashton

Sir William Kt.

Alice
m. 1. Roger
de Moelys,
d. 1323
m. 2. Sir
John
Daumarle

Alice   Joan   Isolda

Clarice   William   Gilbert
             Wibbery

             John   John
             Wotton   Wibbery

Richard Prouz
of Ashton Esq.

John   Thomasin
            m. John
            Chudleigh

William   Richard of
            Ashton

Sir Hugh of
Widworthy, Kt.
m. Alice
Widworthy

Hugh of   William
Widworthy   of Hayford

Julyan m.
Henry Wotton

William   Harry
m. Guildred
d & h. of
Widger

John of Widworthy
m. Ingret Dimock

Alice
m. John Chichester
of Ralegh

William of
Eastervale &
Westervale Esq.
1300 m. Ellen
d. of Jefrey Pont
of Eastervale

William m. Anstice d. & h.
of Reginal Wadacot of
Chagford

John m. Maud
d. & h. of
John Cruwys

1435 John m.
Agnes d. of
Thos Bampfield
of Poltimore Esq.

Richard   Joan m. William
m. Margaret   Butshead
d. & h. of
William Norton
of Newton St.
Cyres

John
m. Joan
d. & heir
of John
Orchard

Lawrence   Christopher   John   Bartholomew   Patrick   Robert   Lawrence   Christopher   Joan
m. Agnes   of Withecombe m. William
d. of Wm.   m. Eleanor   Budokeside
Cole   Sever

John   William   Richard   Katharine
                           m. Trowbridge

De CHAGFORD and WIBBERY
1196-1473

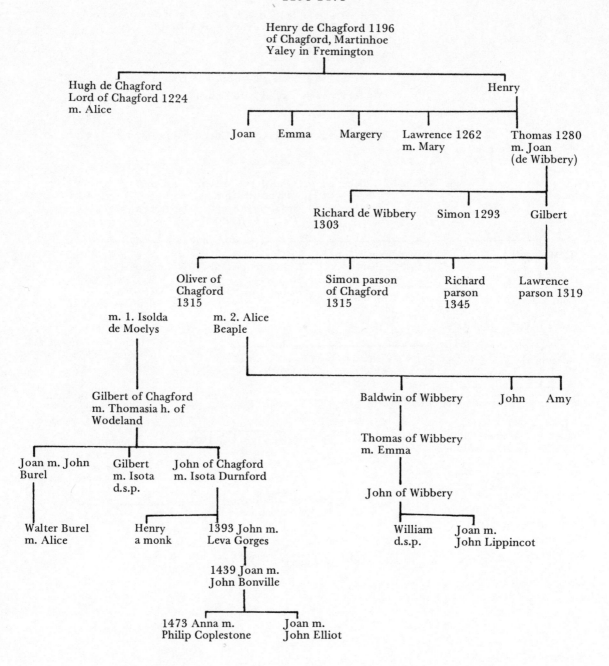

Henry de Chagford 1196
of Chagford, Martinhoe
Yaley in Fremington

- Hugh de Chagford
  Lord of Chagford 1224
  m. Alice
- Henry
  - Joan
  - Emma
  - Margery
  - Lawrence 1262
    m. Mary
  - Thomas 1280
    m. Joan
    (de Wibbery)
    - Richard de Wibbery
      1303
    - Simon 1293
    - Gilbert
      - Oliver of
        Chagford
        1315
        m. 1. Isolda
        de Moelys
        m. 2. Alice
        Beaple
      - Simon parson
        of Chagford
        1315
      - Richard
        parson
        1345
      - Lawrence
        parson 1319

Gilbert of Chagford
m. Thomasia h. of
Wodeland

- Joan m. John
  Burel
  - Walter Burel
    m. Alice
- Gilbert
  m. Isota
  d.s.p.
- John of Chagford
  m. Isota Durnford
  - Henry
    a monk
  - 1393 John m.
    Leva Gorges
    - 1439 Joan m.
      John Bonville
      - 1473 Anna m.
        Philip Coplestone
      - Joan m.
        John Elliot

Baldwin of Wibbery

- John
- Amy

Thomas of Wibbery
m. Emma

John of Wibbery

- William
  d.s.p.
- Joan m.
  John Lippincot

1315. Symon de Wibbebury gives to Oliver de Wybbebury (s. of Gilbert de Wybbebury) and Isolda his wife, the whole of his manor of Chaggeforde, with 'vasto in more de Dertemore', and the Advowson of the Church.

From T.D.A. 1893
Rev. T. W. Whale

BONVILLE
1374-1550

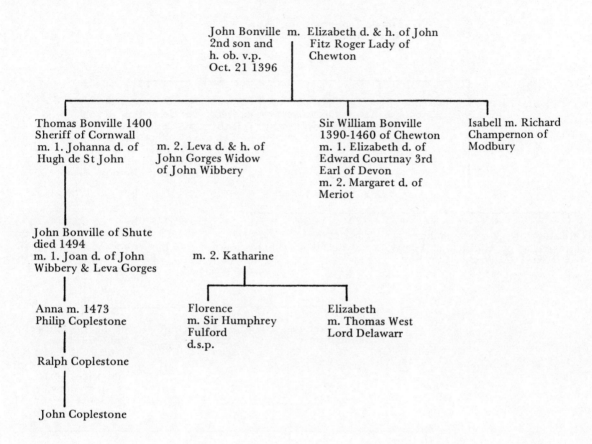

John Bonville m. Elizabeth d. & h. of John
2nd son and   Fitz Roger Lady of
h. ob. v.p.   Chewton
Oct. 21 1396

Thomas Bonville 1400
Sheriff of Cornwall
m. 1. Johanna d. of   m. 2. Leva d. & h. of
Hugh de St John   John Gorges Widow
                         of John Wibbery

Sir William Bonville
1390-1460 of Chewton
m. 1. Elizabeth d. of
Edward Courtnay 3rd
Earl of Devon
m. 2. Margaret d. of
Meriot

Isabell m. Richard
Champernon of
Modbury

John Bonville of Shute
died 1494
m. 1. Joan d. of John   m. 2. Katharine
Wibbery & Leva Gorges

Anna m. 1473
Philip Coplestone

Florence
m. Sir Humphrey
Fulford
d.s.p.

Elizabeth
m. Thomas West
Lord Delawarr

Ralph Coplestone

John Coplestone

COPLESTONE

1384-1550

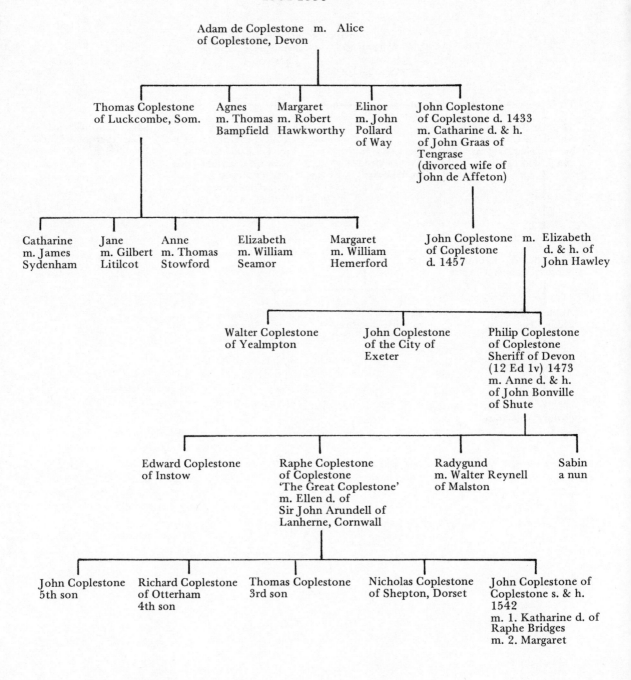

Adam de Coplestone m. Alice
of Coplestone, Devon

- Thomas Coplestone of Luckcombe, Som.
- Agnes m. Thomas Bampfield
- Margaret m. Robert Hawkworthy
- Elinor m. John Pollard of Way
- John Coplestone of Coplestone d. 1433 m. Catharine d. & h. of John Graas of Tengrase (divorced wife of John de Affeton)

Children of Thomas Coplestone of Luckcombe:
- Catharine m. James Sydenham
- Jane m. Gilbert Litilcot
- Anne m. Thomas Stowford
- Elizabeth m. William Seamor
- Margaret m. William Hemerford

John Coplestone of Coplestone d. 1457 m. Elizabeth d. & h. of John Hawley

- Walter Coplestone of Yealmpton
- John Coplestone of the City of Exeter
- Philip Coplestone of Coplestone Sheriff of Devon (12 Ed 1v) 1473 m. Anne d. & h. of John Bonville of Shute

- Edward Coplestone of Instow
- Raphe Coplestone of Coplestone 'The Great Coplestone' m. Ellen d. of Sir John Arundell of Lanherne, Cornwall
- Radygund m. Walter Reynell of Malston
- Sabin a nun

- John Coplestone 5th son
- Richard Coplestone of Otterham 4th son
- Thomas Coplestone 3rd son
- Nicholas Coplestone of Shepton, Dorset
- John Coplestone of Coplestone s. & h. 1542 m. 1. Katharine d. of Raphe Bridges m. 2. Margaret

Chapter Four

CHAGFORD CHURCH

THE CHURCH is the oldest of Chagford's surviving buildings. It stands as witness to the generations who were baptized, wed and buried in it; as its neighbour, the old cross tree, probably stood service before.

The origins of the church are as shrouded in uncertainty as is the early development of Christianity. Each new development or influx of people brought a change of ideals, religion and ritual that evolved into present-day beliefs. The ideals of an invading culture, mingled with the local beliefs of those already settled, contributed to each change, stone circles were succeeded by granite crosses, until someone came to raise a chapel or perhaps a wooden church on the site where our church stands. Over the centuries succeeding generations rebuilt, enlarged, improved and altered it, but despite the changes, the instructions from a higher authority, even the changing names, there is a continuity of birth to death whose centre is the church. Celtic pilgrims, Roman legions, Saxon farmers, Norman knights, and the people whose ancestry stretched back into Stone-Age Dartmoor, all contributed to its foundation.

There is no record of the first building of the church: perhaps a sacred grove or old meeting-place came to house a wooden chapel until the prosperity of tin mining and the mood of the times prompted the more adventurous and permanent structure of stone. St. John's Well, near the church, was a baptismal well until it was filled in during the 1950s. It may have been an early holy or magic site or an early source of water for the community.

The medieval years saw the largely tribal unit that was the manor evolve into the parish of individual families; as this occurred Church and State were busy carving out for themselves their respective areas of influence. The lot of most people was to fall between the ordinations of the Church and the law of the State.

In most cases, and this is almost certainly true of Chagford, the church was built by the lord of the manor and was part of his feudal property. Since tithes must be paid to the church, in the early days it was the lord who collected them. Slowly the Church of Rome tried to bring the property and control of the parish churches under her own control.

Rome was not entirely successful; the patronage of the living remained in private hands in Chagford until the present time, the rector's tithes were collected by the incumbent and not by the bishop, and the glebe lands remained the property of the patron. In addition, the administration of the parish church and its material possessions was in the care of the churchwardens, men chosen from the parish to serve for a year as trustees of the goods and wealth of the church.

The church was almost certainly built by the de Chagfords and the advowson, or right to introduce the rector, was the possession of the lord of the manor until the 17th century. They endowed the living with land which in 1680 amounted to about 60 acres. The incumbent held the glebe for as long as he was rector, it then reverted to the patron. The rector also collected the tithes of the parish, apart from those that were set aside for the maintenance of the church and the care of the poor.

The church seems to be sited at the base of the Chagford Manor. Whether the site had been used for religious purposes before we cannot know, but whatever remnants of bygone ages might have been below the church or occupying its site, they must have been long forgotten when Bishop Bransecombe rode into Chagford to dedicate its church. That was in 1261 and we can only speculate on what the church he dedicated consisted of, and how long it had stood. It was probably built during the early years of the tin boom, which started in the 1160s. Henry de Chagford held the manor in 1196; it might well be he who built the church.

In 1261 it must have been a single-aisled nave with a projecting chancel at the east end, but in the ensuing years tin and agricultural wealth led to its enlargement and decoration. For a brief period Dartmoor was the tin centre of Europe, the Teign valley a major centre of production. Tithes were paid by tinners, and the church itself owned and worked several mines, with the result that by the end of the 15th century the church had grown into a three-aisled building with tower and chancel, and the inclusion of two chapels at the eastern end of the side aisles.

In the earliest days the church was used not only for services but also for parish events, such as assemblies, miracle plays, pageants, perhaps Morris dancing or the parish feast. Chagford later came to have two houses for these purposes, administered by the churchwardens.

In the early days of Chagford church, the families who held the manor and advowson often also provided the rector. Families in Norman times were larger and more like a clan, whose members came first for any consideration. The family of Prouz went into the female line with Dame Alice, who married first Roger de Moelys and second John Daumarle. She had the patronage of Gidleigh and Aveton Giffard, to whom she introduced Simon de Wyberry, a member of her son-in-law's family, while her son, John Daumarle, introduced Richard de Chagford to the living of Gidleigh. The patronage of Chagford had passed to the Wibberys in 1299 along with the manor, and it is this family who provide the first two rectors whose names we know.

Two de Folfordes also hold the benefice, members of the great Norman family from Dunsford; perhaps in this case there was some blood tie also, or one of those complex feudal relationships of obligation that could make a man's fortune.

At that time there seems to be no reason why a man should not be both a priest and a knight. The Crusades, the French Wars and the ideals of chivalry provided a situation where religion and warfare walked happily hand in hand. Knights were prone to spend all night vigils in churches, their sword on the altar, before a battle or major combat. Perhaps Chagford's rectors, Sir Simon de Wyberry, Sir Henry de Folforde, Sir Thomas de Folforde, Sir John Tolthorpe, and others rode into Chagford on their dust-covered horses, their arms rattling at their sides, pulled off their helmets, revealing perhaps a tonsured head, and gave thanks at the altar for their return, while they might be taking mass from the same altar on the morrow.

Certainly there were several leaves of absence: Sir Henry de Folforde for two years, 1328–30; Sir Thomas de Folforde in 1371 for one year; John Depphull for one year in 1392. These are the years of the French Wars, and although these knights were given leave of absence from their flock to study, it rings a little hollow. The Hundred Years War against the French absorbed the wealth, lives and attention of the English for over a century and may have absorbed Chagford's rectors also. But Christian ideals were high, and these men may have been devout priests and brave warriors.

The years of anarchy at the end of the 14th century provide an incident that suggests that the authority of the Church was also subject to unrest. In 1380 Bishop Thomas de Brantygham excommunicated those people who attacked and molested the Archdeacon of Totnes and his officers in the graveyard at Chagford. The bishop does not record the names of the malefactors, perhaps because he was unable to find them out, but this was also the year when young Henry Folforde was accused with others of rioting in Chagford and attacking a sergeant-at-arms (an officer of the crown), and hindering him and his servants in the arrest of certain malefactors, perhaps the very ones that attacked the archdeacon. Thomas Folforde was rector of Chagford at that time, and a relative of the young Henry, but what part he played in the business goes unrecorded.

The next century saw most of the building of the present church. The north and south aisles, the late-Gothic pillars on their octagonal bases that construct the nave, the east window and the windows of the aisles were erected in this period. The tower is 15th century and was still being completed when the churchwarden's accounts began in 1480.

Only two features of the church pre-date this time. The west window of the tower is 13th-century and was probably taken from the west end of the original nave and worked into the base of the tower when the church was being enlarged.

The other is a Norman font which was discovered buried in the floor of the church in 1865. A font had been erected in 1672 of Portland stone, but in 1865 this was being replaced by one in granite. The workmen discovered a far earlier font, buried beneath the one then standing, and presumably its predecessor, but it was broken in the process of removing it and the pieces buried in the rectory garden, that is the garden of Chagford House, at that time still the rectory. However, some descriptions of it remain, and current opinion dates it as 12th-century. In the absence of any further evidence we can suppose that it was the font of the original church.

It was the aim of medieval church builders to provide enough light, and the interior of the church was plastered and painted white, while the windows were tall and graceful.

The services were in Latin and the churchwarden's accounts were written in a form of medieval Latin which legal documents also employed. They begin in 1480, at the time when churchwardens were only just beginning to take office. The Middle Ages saw the increase of the wealth of the Church, and her authorities were at pains to protect Church property from squandering individuals. This was the function of the churchwardens, who were elected for one year as trustees of the goods and chattels of the parish church. Their function was to administer this property; they saw to the upkeep of the church itself, were guardians of its contents and of the churchyard. They built and cared for the Church House, they collected the pence from the parish, animals given to the church were in their charge, as were the church's tin mines, and in these respects they acted as the officers of the church and her estate.

Their accounts record almost every detail of their efforts, their building and repairs, their farming, their tinning, the upkeep of the church's ornaments, and all the minute financial transactions which were required of an organisation that was at the heart of parish life. They begin: 'Chageford Ancint Parish. The account of John Jurston and William Forde, guardians of the goods and chattels of the Store of Blessed Mary of the Chapel in the same place'.

From this faltering beginning until 1600 the churchwardens give a full account of themselves. From their records a vivid picture emerges of an isolated rural community, moulding themselves with characteristic stubbornness to the demands of the time.

The parish church, as the central organisation of the community, benefited from wealth accumulated by its members. While its spiritual function was administered by the rector and intermittent chaplains, its material function was dealt with by the wardens. These seem to be elected from among the more responsible parishioners and are divided into separate guilds to serve different needs. The Four Men were in charge, as time passed they came to adminster all the finances of the other wardens. They collected money from the four quarters of the parish, they managed the church's extensive tin works, they collected sheep, along with the occasional cow or pig, and saw to their management.

The residue of the church's wardens had functions that alter with time. One of the principal sources of revenue for the church was the brewing and selling of ale, and wardens existed for this purpose; the wardens of the Hoggenstore, the wardens of St. Katharine's and the wardens of the Young Men's Store all earned their income by this method.

The wardens of the Store of the Blessed Virgin Mary began by building their chapel and then maintaining it. The wardens of the Store of St. Michael the Archangel, to whom the church is dedicated, looked after the interior of the church. The wardens of St. Nicholas, St. Anthony, St. Elegins, St. George, St. Lawrence, St. Mary, and St. James seem to have had altars to these many saints and taken care of their maintenance.

St. Katharine was the patron saint of tinners. No wonder the Store of St. Katharine Virgin was such a large fraternity, keeping St. Katharine's house for the feast they held on that saint's day, and brewing ale for the feast, and also to raise money. They employed a chaplain to say prayers for the souls of the fraternity, sometimes on the saint's day and sometimes, if seems, throughout the year. They went through a period of intense prosperity, when their members came from several neighbouring parishes, and then diminished with the decline of the tin industry and the impact of Protestantism. There were, in addition, way wardens and market wardens, as these subjects also became the responsibility of the parish.

The period covered by these accounts is one of the most intense upheavals in the religious life of England. The Dissolution of the Monasteries affected Chagford only in providing a chaplain called Richard Splate, who was paid 53s. 4d. in 1539 as half a year's wages. The Dissolution left many monks with no home or job, and farming them out to parish churches was one way of coping with them.

During the first four years of Edward VI's reign the churchwardens kept no account, and this is the period when the church was forced into a Protestant simplicity which Edward's own Protestant education demanded. Only six years later the young king died and his Catholic sister, Mary, came to the throne. Consequently the next year, 1554, the churchwardens spent 20d. on setting up the altar and 4d. for re-hanging the pictures. In fact, so many alterations and repairs were needed that the parishioners borrowed one half thousand-weight of white tin from John Whyddon, which they paid back over the next three years. This was then worth £12 10s. 0d. of lawful money of England.

Little did they then know that Queen Elizabeth's education resembled her brother's and not his sister's, and that her right to accession to the throne rested on Protestant argument and that when she became queen they would have to take down the images, buy a Communion Book and a Communion Table, a Psalter Book and the paraphrase of Erasmus. They would also be required to pay someone to write out a bill and lay it before the Queen's commissioners. In fact, Elizabeth came to the throne in 1558, Chagford re-erected its images in 1559, perhaps seeking to be in line with the times, and then took them down in 1560, presumably discovering their mistake.

However, by that time they had acquired a new source of revenue by buying the right to the fairs and markets from Mr. Copelstone, although they paid Sir John Whyddon for it, which suggests that that gentleman had already rented from Mr. Coplestone the manor and advowson he later came to own in full.

The reign of Elizabeth gives numerous mentions of soldiers, spears, arrows and uniform. The war with Spain and fighting in Ireland, that touched Devon so closely, obviously made itself felt in Chagford, and the village may actually have provided men for the war along with their contribution of arms, uniform and transport. But the changing fortunes of kings and queens were not the primary concern of Chagford church and its people. Like any estate it had buildings to maintain, animals to farm, and the additional wealth of tin to be utilised.

Tithes were paid to the rector in kind, and these, along with the revenue he received from the gift of the patron, supported him. He had the use of the parsonage house, with its stables and gardens, dairy and larder. This house disappeared long since, but stood at one time to the south of the church, in the field surrounding Chagford House.

The parish church collected the small tithes, mostly sheep or small money sums, along with the tithe of a spade penny that every tinner paid. It was also fortunate in being left gifts in the wills of the parishioners, which contributed handsomely to its fortunes. This income, along with that made from ale and tin, allowed the church to grow and to be continually repaired and beautified.

Along with the church itself, there were also the Church House, later belonging to the Whyddons, and now the *Three Crowns,* and St. Katharine's House, both of which were owned and maintained by the church. It seems that originally they were constructed and maintained by the churchwardens for the activities of their various stores and that later they were rented out, the Church House coming to be the residence of the Whyddons, and St. Katharine's House becoming briefly Poddicomb House, due to the residence there of a certain Nicholas Poddicomb.

It was during the reign of Elizabeth that the churchwardens took responsibility for mending the roads and bridges of the parish, and also at this time that provision was made for the poor, who previously had been taken care of by the monasteries. Money was dispensed to sick children, pardoners, wounded soldiers, and others.

In 1569 the churchwardens bought a book for registering christenings, weddings and burials, a sign of increasing organisation. The wardens often had to pay 2d. to 4d. for the writing of the accounts, which was quite apparently a tricky affair, medieval Latin being the language and inconsistent spelling and poor arithmetic being common features.

Another fact tends to confuse the accounts in the early days; each store ran its own account from the festival of its own saint, with the result that their separate accounts may end months apart, or even in a different year.

The bishop visited once a year and this always cost the village several shillings, for his time and perhaps for his entertainment. This may be the origin of the name of the Bishop's House, where he may have stayed, or at least dined. Later, in Queen Elizabeth's reign, her commissioners frequently visited the West Country, and the Four Men were forced to go to Exeter and give an account of themselves. Perhaps this kind of interference made people reluctant to be churchwardens, for it is only during Elizabeth's reign that there are frequent records of fines imposed on those who refused to hold the office.

Apart from providing the necessary vestments, books, candles, bread and wine, the churchwardens had the endless task of keeping the church in good repair. Between 1482 and 1484 the Chapel of the Blessed Virgin Mary was completed, although a window seems to have been added in 1532. Work was still not completed on the tower until 1513, and a new set of bells was hung in 1537 when four old bells were sold. This transaction was incredibly costly and required heavy borrowing from members of the parish. At a time when a labourer might earn 2d. for a day's work the churchwardens borrowed £27.10s. 9d. from various members of the parish, sold four bells for £35 15s. 10d., and spent £55.11s. 7d. on new bells. This money they paid to the auditors of our Lord the Ring. This is the time of the Dissolution of the Monasteries and the suggestion is that the bells might come from a dissolved monastery and were being sold off either by the bishop's auditors or by those of the king. In 1574 a 'wedther cock' was put up on the tower. The clock is mentioned from the earliest accounts in 1488.

A plumber was often employed to mend the lead on the roof, and thatch, timber and shingles were common purchases. The bells were constantly repaired, bell collars, ropes, and the bells themselves required almost yearly attention. The hedge, wall, and gates of the churchyard were repaired, the chapels and interior of the church were plastered and washed with lime, which cost in 1535, two shillings for three sacks.

An organ was in the church, and this, too, needed attention. In 1527, fourpence was paid 'to an aged man who played on the organs here'.

The contents of the church had to be cleaned and repaired, while generous gifts increased the church's goods. These included a Communion Table and various altars (depending on the prevailing religion), surplices, veils, girdles, linen, banners, a crucifix, a chest, viols, pictures, images, lamps, candlesticks, towels, the clock, tapers, a church missal, a bible, an altar cloth, candleabra, and later a manual, two processionals, a hymnal, a psalter, and song books. Later still the Paraphrase of Erasmus and the Desputation of Doctor Jules Hardyn were added.

A list of objects in the care of the ale wardens in 1570 records the safe keeping of tin platters, a broche and andyer, a brandyse of iron, two keffes (vats for brewing), one chetyll (cauldron for brewing), one register book, one ladder, and one tin bottle. The church also owned a silver chalice.

The church's income from tin increased steadily in the 16th century. The tin works at Bubhyll, which the church had managed since the accounts began, were bought by them in the 16th century. They also owned a good flock of sheep, which they rented out to various farmers. They made malt for brewing; they sold grass from the churchyard; they owned several pigs, occasionally a cow. They also paid a man named Thomas Thewle for killing a fox.

When war threatened they provided arrows and quivers and also spears. They employed a holy water carrier. In 1482 with characteristic superstition they paid 4d. to William Tavner for ringing when it thundered, and in 1488 so great was their fear they paid 2d. for ale at the time of the thunder. Ale was a requisite for any job; it had to be provided for the workmen and their helpers if any work was to be completed.

Much of the church's prosperity was dependent on the generosity of the parishioners. The following is an extract from 1492 from the Store of the Blessed Virgin Mary:

> One pair of pigs received from the legacy of Joan Wavyt . . . and so there is due in all 11s. 0d. which is delivered to John Jurston and Henry Addiscott and so the old Wardens are acquitted; and a pair of pigs.

Although the church was the centre of the parish there were also three chapels attached to the manors of Teigncombe, Great Week and Rushford. The chapel at Teigncombe was dedicated to St. Julia. William le Moyne (Monk) was granted the right to a chapel at Rushford in 1329, by Bishop Grandisson. It was a descendant of this family, George Monk, born here in 1608, who restored Charles II to his throne.

Rushford's chapel was taken down by Major Hore in the 18th century, because it obscured the prospect of his house. He used the stones to rebuild his garden and orchard walls, and many of these stones can be recognised in the orchard wall today.

The church owned several fields: Rose Pyke, Forsepyk, St. Katharine's Hay, and another which is not named.

Tin works mentioned as providing church revenue include Bubhyll, Taw Marshe, Cherebroke, Katharine Beme, Clinkyn More, Brodemershe, Labthorn, Cross Parke, Vussedown, Shylston Beme, Colherin, Conyball, and Colham.

The wardens also held 33 polls of writing with the charters of the fairs and markets, which they had purchased. Sadly, these were apparently burnt, in a later fire in the town.

The churchwarden's accounts temporarily ended in 1600. Much of the contents of their accounts is not specifically about the church, but rather the life of the community. The decline of the feudal manor and the importance of the church were matched in national life by the power of Rome and the wealth of the monasteries. This was the situation which led to the intense religious upheavals of the 16th century, and made England a Protestant nation and Chagford a Protestant church. The prosperity, the wealth, the importance, and the security of the parish church in late medieval and Tudor times came to a second flowering in the Victorian age, and each time was succeeded by a decline. But in those halcyon days when King Hal and his red-headed daughter ruled the land, its people looked to the church for guidance, succour and support as truly as a child does to its mother.

RECTORS OF CHAGFORD

1315	Simon de Wyberry	1555	John Staughton
1319	Lawrence de Wyberry	1618	John Dynham
1328	Henry de Folforde		German Gouldstone
	Thomas de Folforde, exchanged benefices with:	1655	John Coplestone
		1662	George Hayter
1382	Sir John Tolthorpe, exchanged benefices with:	1701	George Hayter
		1680	William Reade
1384	Sir Robert Burgeys	1729	Thomas Rennell
1391	Sir William Mayow, exchanged benefices with:	1742	Joshua Hayter
		1771	Joshua Worth
1392	Sir John Dypphull	1779	John Hayter
1397	Lawrence Haukyn	1810	William Moore
1397	John Lydeford	1819	George Hayter Hames
1429	Robert Chirbury, exchanged benefices with:	1821	William Hames
		1852	Hayter George Hames
1434	Michael Lerchdekne	1886	Gerald Lewis Henry Ley
1440	Sir William Forde	1912	Hubert Charles Studdy
1447	Thomas Coplestone	1916	Thomas Collins Walters
1470	Richard Stoyle	1922	Thomas Morgan Bell-Salter
	Henry Grymstone	1931	Cecil Frederick Joy Holmes
1490	Edward Wylichby	1939	Charles Egerton Chadwick
1508	William Trugg	1948	Ralph Sadleir
1517	Robert Becansawe	1953	Alexander Goudge
1525	Robert Weston	1959	Cuthbert Harold Septimus
1539	Francis Coplestone		Buckmaster
	Robert Harneman	1973	George Syers
1555	Robert Fissher	1977	William Bulley

MEDIEVAL RECTORS AND PATRONS

	Rector	Date	Patron
Chagford	Simon de Wyberry	1315	Oliver de Wyberry
	Laurence de Wyberry	1319	Oliver de Wyberry
	Sir Henry de Folforde	1328	
Gidleigh		1324	Lady Alice de Moelys
		1347	Lady Alice de Moelys
	Sir Richard de Chaggeforde	1368	Sir John Daumarle

Medieval Rectors and Patrons—*continued*

	Rector	Date	Patron
Lustleigh		1309	Sir William le Prouz
		1338	Oliver de Wybbery
		1349	Gilbert (son of Oliver) de Wyberry
Aveton Giffard	Sir Simon de Wyberry	1329	Dame Alice de Moelys
	Sir Clement de Folforde	1332	Dame Alice de Moelys
		1358	Sir John Daumarle
		1376	Sir John Daumarle

CHURCH BELLS, 1537

	£	s.	d.
Money borrowed from:			
Richard Batye	4	0	0
Chapel of St. Julia at Teigncombe	4	0	0
Chapel of St. Mary of Weke	1	0	0
William Seryll	1	6	8
John Newcomb	1	5	0
Godfrey Loskew	1	0	0
John Loskew		13	4
William Noseworthye	1	0	0
John Frenshe	1	0	0
William Hore	1	0	0
Stephen Benet	1	0	0
Godfrey Colyhall		15	0
John Peryman, Sen.		10	0
Michael Well		10	0
Thomas Northecote		13	4
Store of St. Mary	1	15	0
John Seynthull		7	6
	£21	15	10

INSCRIPTIONS ON THE CHURCH BELLS

Treble 'Hear me when I call.'
Rev. H. G. Hames, Rector.
J. Hooper, Churchwarden. 1877.
Recast 1914.

2. Rev. H. G. Hames, Rector 1877.
J. Hooper, Churchwardens.
Recast 1914.

3. Thomas Bilbie, Collumpton, fecit 1766.
Recast 1914.

4. 'God preserve the Church and King.'
T. Bilbie, fecit 1766.
Recast 1914.

5. Mr. J. C. and Mr. J. E., Churchwardens.
Thomas fecit 1766.
Recast 1914.

6. Mr. John Coniam and Mr. John Ellis, Churchwardens.
T.B. fecit 1766.
Recast 1914.

7. Mr. John Hooper and Mr. John Wills, John Sarell, W.S. Sidesmen 1766,
T.B. fecit 1766.
Recast 1914.

Tenor 'I to the Church the living call and to the grave do summon all.'
Mr. Joshua Hayter, Rector, Mr. Coniam and Mr. John Ellis, Churchwardens 1766.
This peal was being recast when the Great European War broke out, 1914.
C. G. Hayter Hames, T. Amery, Churchwardens.

Chapter Five

TIN MINING IN THE TEIGN VALLEY

WHEN GRANITE INTRUSION began the creation of Dartmoor 290 million years ago, the process also gave up minerals in solution. In fissures and faults in the granite, layers of precious metals took several million years to crystallise out.

As weathering removed the sedimentary rocks still overlying the granite, the uppermost deposits of minerals were removed.

Since, of all the minerals present—that is iron, zinc, lead, copper, and tin—the latter had the highest temperature of crystallisation and therefore was deposited nearest the granite, it was predominantly tin that remained on the moor proper. Apart from tin lodes running along the faults and fissures of the surface, lumps of ore might be broken off by weathering and washed down into the gravel river beds and banks, becoming the tin stone of the streams and rivers. Some of this tin stone, along with the parent lodes, was now hidden beneath peat and growan or running sharply into the hillsides under the surface of the rock.

Stone Age man must have roamed these hillsides, hunting game with flint tools for thousands of years before knowledge of copper working, and shortly afterwards the discovery of bronze, crept into the area. The extent of the prehistoric remains, from the early Bronze Age to the Iron Age, on the high slopes of the North and South Teign, an area rich in tin, leaves little doubt that the lodes found in the river bed were utilised by local smiths. The origin of the name Teign may be connected to that of the metal. To what extent tin was ever exported from the Chagford area in pre-Norman times, either raw or worked into precious objects, we are not likely to discover.

The Roman Empire received much of its tin from the mines of Northern Spain, although it seems likely that it was being shipped from Cornwall to the Mediterranean at least throughout the Iron Age. The Phoenicians were said to have come to Cornwall for tin. Diodurus (*c.* 40 B.C.) said that the men of Belerium (the most western part of Cornwall) cast the tin into giant knuckle-bones for exportation. One of these has been found and resides now in Truro museum. Whether any of this tin was brought down from Devon to the shipping point of St. Michael's Mount, we do not know.

After the collapse of the tin mines in Spain in the middle of the 3rd century A.D., the south-west of England had a virtual monopoly of tin in Europe. The tin from our region was also said to be of higher quality and greater purity than any other then known. The Romans, however, appear to have been unaware of tin deposits on Dartmoor, although towards the end of their occupation of England they made some attempt at mining Cornish tin.

When the Romans withdrew, the West Country reverted to the tribal kingdom of Dumnonia, whose royal residence was at Gelliwig, later at Caerynyddawg, thought to be Callington, to the west of the Tamar. From here was ruled a people speaking a branch of Gaelic called Brythonic and worshipping a god named Beli under the auspieces of the Queen of Nature. These were the people among whom King Arthur rode, and it is hard to imagine that they did not use the metals of the area, when they were a people noted for the quality of their metalwork.

As the Saxons moved into Devon, these hill people moved away, leaving only a few isolated farmsteads around the edge of the moor. Perhaps they left a few native smiths to supply the newcomers with their needs, or perhaps a worker of metals was too precious a member of the community for the tribe to move without him. Yet perhaps some overlap of religion, for the area was already infiltrated with Christians, left the possibility of co-operation.

Lydford emerged during the period of the Saxon kings, second only to Exeter as the earliest of Devon's towns. Lydford was later to become the focus for the mining industry in Devon and it would be interesting to know if tin really was connected with its foundation. Coins were minted at Lydford during the reigns of Ethelred II, Canute, Harold I, and Edward the Confessor, and the town was laid waste after the Conquest. Domesday put Lydford into the hands of the king; later it became the centre of the Duchy of Cornwall in Devon.

Domesday records nothing of metal-working or mining in this area and, after the Conquest of 1066, another century would elapse before the Norman feudal system bit into the potential of the minerals of Dartmoor.

In the second half of the 12th century tin began to be heavily exploited on Dartmoor. It is possible that Jews may have been in some way responsible for the upsurge of the industry. Blowing-houses, where the raw material was smelted into pure tin, were apparently known as Jews' houses. Also, in 1198 William de Wrotham, Sheriff of Devon, called a jury of 26 'wise and discreet' men in full County Court in Exeter and asked them upon oath 'what was the just and ancient weight of the City of Exeter by which anciently now and at all times the second smelting of tin was wont to be made'. These would be men who were involved in the industry and could declare its normal usage, and among the names of the jurors are Roger Rabi and Eli Mewi.

This court was the first Convocation or Parliament of Tinners where the laws and practices of the Stannaries were discussed and ordained. Later Convocations met on the top of Crockern Tor where they sat on seats of stone around a granite table.

From the 12th century onwards tax was paid to the king on all smelted tin before it could be sold. This was known as tin coinage and it soon became necessary to appoint officers to collect the tax and courts where the metal could be weighed and stamped, after the quality was checked and the duty paid.

In 1201 King John granted to the Tinners of Devon and Cornwall a charter giving them free status, an act of such generosity it can only reflect the potential wealth the king hoped to realise from the promotion of the industry within his royal forest, for the tinners had to pay rent for their mines or streamworks to the owner of the land. Chagford must have become a stannary town quite naturally as the centre of the Teign valley area, and a place from which the heavy metal could be transported along the King's Way to Exeter, the nearest city and port.

In 1305 Edward I granted two charters which confirmed and defined the rights of tinners. The Stannary Courts of Devon were to be held at Chagford, Ashburton and Tavistock; tinners offending against the law were to be tried only by the Stannary Courts and imprisoned only at Lydford Castle. Tinners were confirmed as free men and were further exempted from tallages, tolls, stallages and aids. The only tax from which they were not exempt was the lay subsidy, which was a tax of a tenth or a fifteenth of the value of the taxpayers' possessions sometimes voted to the king by parliament. The next charter of 1327 exempted them from this tax also.

There were obvious advantages in being a tinner, but there were also costs. Toll tin had to be paid by the tinner to the owner of the land; this was paid in Devon by one-tenth of the profit of the tinworks, so that if the tinner made no profit the freeholder suffered accordingly. This, of course, meant that the Duchy of Cornwall, which was granted Dartmoor Forest in 1239, was receiving toll tin from all the tinners working within its bounds. Within the parishes tinners paid a shovel penny in tithes to the church and paid toll tin to the freeholders of the land on which they worked.

From the beginning there was some confusion about who was a tinner and who was not. A succession of Norman legislation attempted to define those persons who were eligible for the special privileges and duties of a tinner, and in what circumstances the common law of England applied to them. The 1305 Charter stipulated that they should be under the jurisdiction of the Stannary Courts only with the exception of pleas of life, land and mayham.

At times there was considerable ill-feeling between the local community and the tinners, who quickly became a separate and, in some ways, elite group. Not that tinning was an easy life, the veins of metal were pinched, faulted and cracked, while profits might be considerable for some months, a lode might disappear or dive under shelves of granite where Norman technology could not reach it. The work was hard and the weather unkind, squabbles broke out between tinners about water courses and bounds, smelting cost them money, tax must be paid, and tin could only be sold at coinage time, which happened at most four times a year.

The old records speak of 'tinners and adventurers', a good term to describe the kind of men that prospecting seemed to attract. Free status was not so easy to come by in the 12th and 13th centuries; if a Chagford villein could escape his farm duties, mark out for himself a prospecting area on the moorland slopes and succeed in drawing tin from it, he had not only found a source of income no other local employment could provide, he had also risen in status and freed himself from the bonds of villeinage. He was his own man.

Methods varied slightly, but the basic utensil was water. Not only were many free-lying lumps of tin-ore found in the streams, but if water ran through material containing tin-ore, the metal would be deposited on the bed, while the soil and gravel were carried away. For this reason the process was known as tin streaming, and it was only much later, when surface supplies had been heavily worked, that any form of shaft mining developed.

A—Stream. B—Ditch. C—Mattock. D—Pieces of turf. E—Seven-pronged fork.
F—Iron shovel. G—Trough. H—Another trough below it. I—Small wooden trowel.

Fig. 3. Tin Streaming, a 16th-century illustration showing part of the process of tin
extraction. (*Georgii Agricolae*, Book VIII)

Tin streaming is little more than panning, and 'the old men' may also have found small quantities of gold, silver, perhaps lead, zinc, or copper. By throwing the surface material into a fast-running stream, raking away the debris of wood and vegetation and retrieving the tin stone from the bed of the stream they separated the metal from its surroundings. Then they would divert the water-course sufficiently to work over a new patch of ground.

Tin bounding must have grown out of some ancient custom, and was probably a result of a sparse population in a metaliferous area. In a densely-populated area it would have been impossible. In order to claim the right to work a piece of land for tin it was necessary to bound the area in question. This was done, quite simply, by turning up turves at the corners of the area to be worked, by which a quadrilateral was marked out that was now bounded. The corner markings came to be regulated as piles of six stones. If the area was to be worked continually the bounds had to be renewed a year and a day after their original setting, and thereafter on the same day every year. In the early days of mining the tinner had no need to ask permission of a landowner to pitch bounds, but was given freedom by law to prospect for the metal wherever he wished, excepting churchyards, houses and gardens, and this remained the law until 1574 when tinners were restricted from prospecting in meadows, orchards, outbuildings, and arable land. If the landowner permitted them, they could do so, but they no longer had the free right. Tinners had been a serious pest in preceding years, interfering with farming and causing silting up and damage to rivers. A man called Richard Strode, M.P. for Plympton in 1512, attempted to pass a Bill through parliament to curtail their actions, and found himself in irons in a dungeon in Lydford Castle. He managed to get out by paying a fine to the keeper of the castle, and an Act was passed by parliament which is the origin of the freedom of speech in the House of Commons that exists today.

Out of tin streaming grew the need to find the parent lodes of metal. These could be discovered by divining, by vegetation patterns, or by cutting trenches and then working back along the lodes. As a result the Dartmoor slopes are marked with the remains of streaming and trenchworks; for example, the extensive workings below the *Warren* inn, and probably at one time a large part of Chagford's agricultural land was worked over in this way as well.

At first tinners seem to have been villeins who left the farms for a more adventurous but precarious life. As the industry became more prosperous non-tin-workers would bound works and then lease them to working tinners. In addition yeoman farmers and gentry owned bounds, both on their own land and scattered over the moor, and they would then employ tinners to work it. This naturally led to an increase in the range of persons classed as tinners and caused further confusion in the law.

Chagford church received revenue from the tinworks at Bubhyll from the opening of the accounts in 1480, and throughout the period of the accounts their tin interests increased. In some cases they were left mines in the wills of the parishioners, notably John Westcott, jnr. His will, dated 1522, leaves to the Store of St. Michael a half share of a tin works called Shylston Beme, to the Store of St. Katharine's a half share of a tin works called Bowrehaycomb, and to the Store of St. George a half share of a tin works called Colham, and the Store of High Cross received half of Stenyehylhed and half of Massehays.

It is interesting, also, that he left to one Philip Furze half a tin works called Hyer Colham and half of Hobbhoole, and to one Henry Dennis the other half of the Hyer Colham and half of Lower Colham. Neither Furze nor Dennis is an uncommon name, yet only a decade earlier Philip Furze was the keeper of Lydford prison, who had held Richard Strode, M.P., prisoner, and the deputy Warden of the Stannaries was one Thomas Dennis, who was also involved in the Strode affair. Perhaps John Wescott, jnr., tin-owner, anxious to protect the rights of his heirs, felt it wiser to placate the officials of the Stannaries, and such dealings tend to throw shade on the Devon miners' quest for tin

Tin workings within the parish of Chagford must have been numerous, for one tinner might have many bounds that he worked only intermittently. Chagford's tinners also had bounds on Dartmoor and within other parishes, while the tinners of the entire area of north-eastern Dartmoor were under the jurisdiction of the Chagford Stannary Court.

The remains of the works around *Warren* inn are still very much in evidence; there is mention of tinworks at Cherebroke in the valley of the Dart, and all along the Teign and its tributaries streamworks were opened and trenches dug. They occur from Week to Westcote to Biera; at Shilston (Shylston Beme), Rushford, Corndon, Yardworthy and Dogamarsh, within the neighbouring parishes and on the 'King's Forest of Dertemore' the tinners removed the metal, had it smelted down and brought it into Chagford to be taxed and sold.

There is little doubt that not all the tin worked on Dartmoor found its way into the Stannary Courts; the coinage was 15s. 7½d. per thousandweight of white tin, which is roughly three per cent. of its value. This made selling it illegally well worth while, and in addition a tinner who was hard-up might not wish to wait for the next coinage day to sell his tin and realise his profit.

The Chagford Stannary Court was a building of two floors that stood in the village square. In the upper chamber the pleas of the court were heard by the Steward of the Stannaries before a jury of tinners. Below the tin was brought before the controller and the receiver, with their stamping hammer and weights, and before the assay master together with clerks and officials. The tin was weighed, its quality checked, and the duty paid on it. When it had been checked the Duchy Arms were stamped on it. The identifying mark of the owner was already stamped on to the block, so that there should be no problem of identification. In 1789 a visitor to Chagford was able to record that he had breakfasted in the Stannary Room and had seen the stamp for coining tin, which was a lion rampant between 15 balls in a circle, around it the motto 'Sigillum Ducatus Cornubiae'.

The Stannary weight was also there: 'The Hundred weight, cubical with a bottom like a bowl—on one side the County Arms and Stannary Arms. On another side the Portcullis with a Coronet on it, between two ostrich feathers—on another the King's Arms—On the other the Prince's Coronet and the Rose and Crown-Date obliterated, except a Figure 6. On a smaller weight is a date, 1605'.

The day of the coinage, which was generally held twice yearly, at Michaelmas, 29 September, and at Roodmas or Lady Day, 25 March, would be like a fair, bringing into the town not only the officials of the Crown, the tinners with their wagons of smelted metal, but also merchants from London and abroad, looking to buy tin for their bronze and pewter businesses.

In 1554 the market value of white tin—tin which had been twice smelted and was therefore reasonably pure—was £25 for a hundredweight, which in Devon meant 1,200 lbs. In Cornwall weights, measures and rates of duty were different. To give an idea of the value of a tin works, in 1554 the church in Chagford received £3 1s. 8d. in all from its interests in tin, yet in another year its profits rose to £20, while in some years it bore the cost of tin working and made no profits at all.

In 1513 a tinner working as a labourer in the church's tinworks at Bubhill received sixpence, but there is no indication of how long he had been working. At this time a sheep cost about twelve pence.

To give an idea of comparative prices, in 1502 the church made 7s. 7d. from tin and 5s. 4d. from wool; often the wool brought greater profits than tin-working. In 1503 the church sold a workman's cottage for 20d., and in 1515 they paid John Frynde 4s. for 10 oaks. The cottage may have been in very bad repair, but all the same it was worth less than five oak trees, or two sheep, or four pounds of white tin.

Originally tax was paid on the first smelting of tin and the second had to be made within one of the Stannary towns. With the introduction of blowing-houses tin-stone could be purified in one firing, and from the 13th century onwards the standard coinage procedure in the Stannary towns was established.

Blowing-houses were found all over the moor and consisted of a simple granite building with a thatched roof, containing a large furnace. Water-power was used to operate the bellows which fanned the flames; fuel was primarily peat dug off the moor; and the molten metal reduced in the furnace was run into granite moulds containing between one and two hundredweight of tin. Within the parish of Chagford there were blowing-houses at Thornworthy, at Outer Down, and at King's Oven at the south-west corner of the parish.

Chagford was apparently humming with metaliferous prosperity when Queen Elizabeth I died in 1603. At Michaelmas and Roodmas the town filled with tinners, merchants and officials, and doubtless the inhabitants of the town made certain they reaped some of the harvest passing through. The inns would be busy, horses and wagons would be in demand, the travellers needed food and entertainment. The Stannary Court must have brought to Chagford all the wealth, excitement and prestige of an international town, if only for a few short days. Then in 1617 disaster struck. On 6 March 1617, a Friday as it happened, the Stannary Court was being held in Chagford, presumably for the Roodmas session. A contemporary records the scene: '. . . the late happening at Chagford in Devonshire upon Friday the 6th of March last past upon which day his highnes Court of Stanneryes being holden, the Court set, and great assemblies of Esquires and gentlemen there present, the Jurors called, summoned forth and sworn upon their oaths, without partiality to give upright verdict'.

A case was called and, according to the narrator, the defendant told a story so unlikely that not only the jury but the whole bench 'thought it to be most fabulous' and told the defendant to be careful, for he was under oath. To which he replied that if he lied let the building fall upon his head in just judgement of God upon him. No sooner were the words out of his mouth when the timber and walls of the building simply collapsed, killing many people and injuring 17 more with broken limbs, bruised heads and backs. Certain of the esquires and gentlemen were killed 'and their limbs almost beaten to pieces'. Among these gentlemen was Master Nicholas Eveleigh, Esq., Steward of the Court and his two clerks, John Cleake and Richard Beere. There were also killed one Master Richard Cottle, Esq., Councillor of the Middle Temple in London, two attorneys of the law, Master Timothy Moule, and Master Robert Nilford. Yet apparently amid the rubble and the bodies a small child was found alive and unhurt. Despite the narrator's assurances that this was the judgement of God upon sinners, it is also quite likely that the upper chamber of the building was over-crowded, since it was apparently a special case being heard. The Courthouse was unable to take the strain and collapsed. However, God's judgement on the tinners might easily have been overdue and it is interesting that this occurred when the surface lodes were becoming scarcer and the industry was beginning to decline. Tin continued to be worked in the Chagford parish until the present century, but it had passed its peak.

In the 18th century the process turned to shaft mining and the 'old men' were forgotten. The mining companies now bought themselves prospecting rights, and brought metal out of deep underground tunnels through the assistance of pulleys and wheels. Although the industry still employed a large work force there was no longer the possibility of working alone as an adventurer.

In the 19th century a collection of mines was opened between Hameldown and Hurston Ridge. The Birch Tor and Vitifer complex, the Bushdown Mine, the East Vitifer Mine, Golden Dagger Mine, the King's Oven, and Waterhill Mine, and the West Vitifer Mine were all within an area three miles square, to the west of Hameldown. Of these Bushdown, King's Oven and Waterhill, and the West Vitifer mines were all within the Chagford parish boundaries. The time of their greatest prosperity was the middle of the 19th century (1850–1870) and after that time the lodes became too small to justify the cost and the mines closed down.

One last attempt at tin-mining occurred in the 20th century at Great Week, where, in 1886 the Great Week Consuls Adventurers opened a shaft and produced 55 tons of black tin over the next four years. After this the mine changed hands twice and was last worked in 1904, but apparently never again produced any significant quantity of metal.

With regard to the Stannary Institutions, the Stannary Courthouse was replaced with a two-storey thatched building at the lower side of the square, with market stalls below and the courthouse chamber above. The Steward's Court was held in this chamber as before, but it soon became easier and quicker to sue in the Court of the Vice-Warden of the Stannaries, while the introduction of shaft mining with a few companies employing at the most forty men, led to a decline in the use of Stannary Courts until they were finally abolished, in 1836, by a Act of Parliament.

The Tinner's Parliament, held at their stone table on Crockern Tor, at least until everyone adjourned to Tavistock to get warm, was last held in 1752 and the remains of their stone furniture are now gone. Theoretically such a parliament could meet again, but there is no longer tin, over which statutes might be enacted. The Council of the Duchy of Cornwall is still headed by the Warden of the Stannaries, a far cry from the days of Elizabeth I, when the great Sir Walter Raleigh was in possession of that title. The Stannary Court of Chagford fell into disrepair. By Victorian times it disgraced the town so completely that it was demolished and a new building was erected to take its place.

The tinners have truly gone. Of all the inhabitants of Dartmoor, they have most lastingly scarred it. All over the valleys and slopes of the moor the stream-works, mine-shafts and trenches of the old men remain, while the tin—and the lead, zinc, iron and copper, silver and gold—now are all gone.

Tin Works within Chagford Stannary

Rix Parke, Bubhyl, Cherebroke, Colham, Katharine Beme, Vussedown, Taw Marsh, Crosse Park, Labthorn, Brodemershe, Clinkyn More, Shylston Beme, Colherin, Conyball, two near Chagford Bridge, Lagland, Bowrehaycomb, Bowrehaydown, Stenyehylhed, Massehays, Hobbhoole, Southkyngesmyth, Borycombhedd, Waterdonrygge, Lytlebrodemersch, Southdogmersh.

The Fall of the Stannary Court House

In Chagford 6th March 1617

(Extracted from a pamphlet, 1618, in the Bodleian Library, Oxford)

Concerning Chagford in Devonshire, where by the Fall of the Stannary court house, many good and worshipfull gentlemen received their doomes of hard misfortune, as is verified, which through the cursed imprecation of a perjured wretch fell upon them: therefore with your patience, I will insert some few examples of like feare and mischance, to make the matter itself bring with it a truer touch of trembling terror.

As the name of God it selfe is most glorious, so should we not use it but with trembling and feare, for the Lord saith he shall be pronounced guilty that taketh his name in vaine. As for example, I have read of two young men, making but a jest of God's most glorious name, strived whether of them could sweare most terriblest, or curse most horriblest, but their jesting was so odious in God's sight, that one of them was presently stroken with madnesse, the other with sodaine death. Thus have you heard the reward of profane swearing, and bitter curses, whereby God's holy name is much dishonoured, and the speaker in danger of damnation, whereunto I will now adde the late happening at Chagford in Devonshire upon Friday the 6 of March last past upon which day his highnes Court of Stanneryes being holden the Court set, and great assemblies of Esquires and Gentlemen there present the Jurors Cal'd, summond forth and sworne upon their oathes, without partiality to give upright verdict: being thus charged, falshood must needs be odious both to God and man, and none but graceless wretches will be so impious as to prefer the same unto the Seat of Justice.

But now marke the effect: There was (as it is reported) an evidence brought in by a fellow, to which the Jury gave but little trust, the matter for some special occasion

I leave concealed, and therefore most fitly to be omitted; but too true it is the evidence giver brought in, upon his oath a false accusation, in whose mouth, as it seemed, a forged lye was ready, and there told such an unlikely tale, that not only the Jury but the whole bench thought it to be most fabulous, and therefore with good admonitions bestered him to bee carefull and to take good heed upon what ground he take his oath, yet notwithstanding this audacious fellow destitute of all grace and goodness, thus tempted the Lord's anger, saying, if I sweare amisse (quote he) or if I speake wrongfully, let God I beseech him make me a fearful example to all perjured wretches and that this house wherein I stand, may sodainely fall upon my head, and that the fall thereof may be seen to bee the just judgement of God upon me: Oh wofull wish! O cursed desire! Oh vile tempter of God's anger to solicite heaven to black vengeance! For no sooner were there words spoken, but in short time after, the timber and walls of the house (though seeming strong) the weather faire and cleare, without either storm or tempest, sodainly fell down, whereby in the fall and overthrow of this large timber building, this graceless varlet with divers others, werefore bruised and beaten to death, and the number of seventeen more greviously hurt and wounded, some in their armes, some in their legges, some on their heads, some on their backs, and other parts of their bodies, to the great danger of their lives, and that which is more lamentable to tell, certain Esquires and Gentlemen of good calling, by the fall of the said walls and timber, were sodainly strocke dead, and their limbs almost beaten in pieces, with sodainnesse of death, not only amazed the whole Town, but strooke a trembling feare throughout all the neighbouring villages.

The principall of the Gentlemen which thus tasted of this rigorous hard misfortune, I will here make known. As first, Master Nicholas Eveleigh Esq., Steward of the Court, a Gentleman of much vertue, and well beloved in that country; also his two Clerks, John Cleake and Richard Beere, for whom is made much moane. Likewise, one Master Richard Cottle Esquire, and Councellour of the middle Temple in London. In like manner two Atturneyes of the Law, Master Timothy Moule, and Master Robert Nilford, with some certain others, which felt the heavy burden of God's Judgements, and had their bodies even bruised to pieces, through the invocation of this wicked wretch thus incenting Heavens anger, whom God forgive.

Duely, I must now speake of a wonderfull thing there happening. In the midst of this confused heape of timber, stone and earth, under which so many lay slaughtered, there was a young Childe miraculously preserved, for in the midst of these men of more able strength, which lay bruised and beaten to death, as it were with their brains bashed out, was the same Childe found safe and sound, whereon appeared not so much as the smallest hurt that might be: yet judge we charitably, God onely knows the meanes of this Childes preservation, and the cause of his heavy punishment shewed upon the others.

But now to strike terrour into the harts of the Readers, never was so great woe made in Chagford, for so many good men covered over with the ruins of earth and stone: never were so many Gentlemen of account, Counsellours of worth, Atturneyes and Clerks of the Law, thus at one time brought to unhappy destinie. Some lay starke dead closed up in dust and earth: some wounded with bruised and broken bones:

some crying and calling for helpe: yea, such amazed feare thundered about the whole Towne, that it was marvellous to heare. The neighbouring people came from all the adjoining villages, some crying for one friend, some for another, fathers for children, children for their fathers, husbands for wives, wives for husbands, brothers for brothers, ye nothing but lamentations, rung peales of woe, and such confusion of sorrow possessed the people, that it was pitifull to see.

Thus have you heard how God call downe his irefull hand in this unhappy towne.

1. Scorhill Circle.

2.   Roman Altar, Chagford churchyard.

3.   Week Down Cross, Chagford.

4. Chagford Bridge.

5. Bellacouch, Chagford.

6 & 7. Two carvings beside the east window, Chagford church.

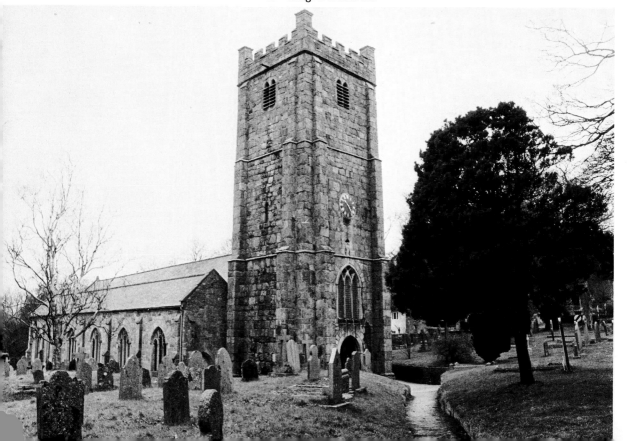

8. Chagford church.

9. Holy Street Mill, Chagford, *c.* 1860.

10. The *Three Crowns* hotel, Chagford, *c.* 1870.

Chagford The subscriptions of the Inhabitants of Chagford as[...] toward[...] propagation of the Gospell in New England

	£	s	d
John Prouz Esq	1	00	00
John Gayhes Clarke	1	00	00
John Rowe gent	0	10	00
John Eveleston gent	00	02	06
John Whyddon Esther gent	00	01	00
John Rowe gent	00	00	00
John Whyddon the younger gent	00	02	06
John Frend	00	02	00
John Vallence	00	02	06
John Voysill	00	00	06
Will Curry	00	00	06
John Rowe	00	00	06
Will Leavell	00	00	06
Rich Frend	00	02	06
Gilbert Northcott	00	00	06
Will Taberner	00	02	00
Henry Hewnworthy	00	02	00
Henry Endacott	00	01	06
Henry Hooper Esher	00	01	00
Gilbert Smith	00	01	00
John Woodley	00	01	00
John Dodd	00	01	00
Andrew Warder	00	00	06
Gregory Dodd	00	01	00
Henry Wills	00	01	00
Richard Warroll	00	01	00
Henry Hooper the younger	00	00	06
Thomas Wills	00	00	06
Rich Worthstake	00	01	00
John Varder	00	00	06
Will Lethbridge	00	00	06
John Jennings	00	00	06
John Baron	00	02	00
Will Lake	00	00	04
Rich Lyne & his father	00	02	00
Will Berriman	00	02	06
Robt Westaway	00	00	06
James Bennett	00	00	06
Benedict Splatt	00	00	06
Walter Yarell	00	01	06
Will Lethbridge	00	10	06
Gregory Hooper	00	00	06
Roger May	00	00	03
Will Paule	00	00	06
John Leavell	00	00	06
Thomas Foster	00	00	06
Robert Ellis	00	00	06
John Bennett	00	00	03
John Nosworthy Hober	00	01	00
William Vallence	00	01	00
Mary Nosworthy	00	00	06
Rich Chidon	00	00	00
Thomas Nosworthy	00	01	00
John Enticott	00	00	00
James Clynell	00	00	06
John Harris			

11. A list, *c.*1650, entitled 'Chagford—the Subscriptions of the Inhabitants of Chagford towards the propagation of the Gospel in New England'.

12. Sidney Godolphin.

13. Thomas Hayter, Bishop of Norwich and London, from an oil painting *c*.1760 at Chagford House.

14. Rushford Tower, Chagford, *c*.1870.

15. Sandy Park, or Dockerman's Bridge, on the Teign (from watercolour sketches by Swete, 1789).

16.   The Old Shambles, Chagford. This was the market building in the Square until its demolition in 1862. The open drain shows in the foreground.

17.   The Old Shambles.

18. James Perrot, the Dartmoor guide.

19. Mrs. Bowden, aged 94.

20. Mill Street, Chagford, with the Square beyond, *c.* 1860.

21. The village blacksmith, Chagford, *c.* 1870.

22. The lower part of the Square, Chagford, at the turn of the century, showing the old forge and the fountain.

23. The first motor bus at the Cross Tree, from an early Edwardian photograph.

24. Queen Victoria's Jubilee celebrations, the Square, Chagford.

25. Sheep market in the Square, Chagford, *c.*1865.

26.   Chagford Archery Society, photographed by G. Ormerod in 1863.

27.   Stanley's memorial stone being taken from Chagford by Mr. Reed's traction engine, 1904.

28.   A Victorian photograph of Mill Street, Chagford, with Mr. Berry's house (now *Moorland's* hotel) on the left.

29.   The Square, Chagford, from Mill Street in early Edwardian times.

30. Rushford Mill, Chagford, with the stepping stones, in the late 19th century.

31. The village dustcart in New Street, from a Victorian photograph.

32. The *Three Crowns* inn, Chagford, at the turn of the century.

33. Chagford from Rushford Wood.

Chapter Six

TUDOR CHAGFORD

IN 1485 the Wars of the Roses ended and Henry Tudor became King Henry VII. In 1492 Columbus reached the New World. Feudalism had reached its end, and the English Rennaissance began.

Such changes touched Devon closely; its ports were developing and its sea-faring families were to provide Queen Elizabeth with some of her most favoured courtiers: Francis Drake, Walter Raleigh, Richard Grenville, and John Hawkins. The growing body of law and administrative work gave a new social position to merchants and yeomen who became lawyers, judges, officials and clerks of a more sophisticated court and government. In this respect we have the life of Sir John Whyddon of Chagford, Judge of the King's Bench, as a clear example.

With the rise of these new families the old feudal lords lost ground. The Courtenays, Earls of Devon for three centuries, forfeited their lands to the Crown under Henry VIII, during the break with Rome; the Bonvilles had died out during the Wars of the Roses and in Chagford the Prouz family had left Gidleigh and taken up residence at Waye Barton, where they had slipped into the role of country gentry. The Coplestones gave up the manor of Chagford during the Tudor period, while the yeomen farmers, merchants and freemen of medieval times became the new gentry of the English Rennaissance.

Feudalism dwindled gently away. During the Middle Ages the ranks of freeholders had grown steadily, while land held by Knight's Service had decreased. By the beginning of the Tudor period the only sizeable quantities of unenclosed land was the moorland, which continued to be encroached upon, where this was possible. The land was now primarily divided into small farms, held by freeholders. The free status of the tinners had contributed to the demise of the villein class, while the cottagers had become tradesmen and wage earners.

At the end of the 15th century, therefore, we find Chagford, still naturally boasting its lords of the manor, but with the land, the real strength and wealth of the parish, belonging to freeholders, who held farms covering the parish.

The coming years were years of intense change and widening horizons. Henry VIII wrested control of the Church out of the hands of Rome and the English Reformation came about. Perhaps most importantly for local people the monasteries were dissolved and the wealth and land of these great institutions became the gift of the king to his favourites. While the people gained some freedom, they also lost the paternal hospitality with which the monks had previously protected the poor, destitute and outcasts.

Prosperity, however, increased. The woollen industry, foreign trade, and the development of the colonies brought wealth to people all over England. In the south-west the tin industry still thrived and the seaports grew and flourished. Agriculture was the basic wealth of Devon, and descriptions of food in the Tudor manor or farmhouse, with their game, their pies, their lavish use of herbs and spices give an indication of the prosperity of the countryside.

Despite its change of leadership, the Church held firm at the centre of the parish. The tithing system saw to the upkeep of the parish church and its incumbent, and bound the parishioners to their focus.

Chagford was a Stannary town throughout this period and was a prosperous little market town bordering the moor and its mineral wealth. While the lordship of the manor had developed away from its feudal origins, it continued, not only as an indication of status, for the lords of the manor were the greater families of the period, but also as bequeathing legal and financial status. Yet the land the manors covered had become a collection of farms or estates, belonging, often freehold, to the gentry and yeomanry of the parish.

The manor of Chagford was in the possession of the Coplestones when Henry VII came to the throne. In 1493 it was given to Margaret, Countess of Richmond, mother of the king. This lady resided at her manor of Great Torrington and the manor of Chagford was held of her by Ralph Coplestone.

The manor of Teigncombe was held by the Bonvilles until the beginning of the period, and became the possession of the Whyddon family in the reign of Elizabeth. The Whyddons also purchased the manor of Chagford from the Coplestones in 1556, along with the patronage of the living. The manor of South Teign, known as the Prince's Manor by virtue of its being the gift of the Prince of Wales, was a large manor including Midlecote, Easton and Great Week, with parts of the parish of Moreton-hampstead. It became the property of the Whyddon family in the time of Sir John Whyddon, the judge, and probably accounts for the siting of Whyddon House near Easton farm. Shapley was in the possession of the family of Prouz from 1292–1639, after which it also came to the Whyddons.

Rushford was held by the Monke family in the Middle Ages, but came to the family of Hore in the Tudor period. The Hores had moved into the area in the time of Richard II and married an heiress of Risford. They were probably responsible for building the Tudor barton of Rushford, which was apparently a fine Tudor barton, standing slightly north of the original Norman manor house. Monk's Withecombe, originally a part of the Rushford manor may get its name from the family of Monk.

The Courtenays held land in Chagford parish intermittently in late medieval and early Tudor times. In 1432 Philip Courtenay was given the lease of the manor of South Teign for 10 years and in 1446 this was increased to a grant for life of the manor and the forest of Dartmoor. The family saw a sharp decline in the time of Henry VIII, but towards the end of the reign Peter Courtenay held the manor of South Teign once more. This land, including Broadeweek, Midlecote and Yardworthy, he sold to William Knapman.

William Knapman was a substantial landowner of the period, also owing Broad-withecombe and Withecombe, along with Rushford Wood. He bought Collerewe from Christopher Coplestone. His daughter married William Northmore, to whom a large part of his property went.

The Northmores of Cleve, in St. Thomas's, Exeter, also came to inter-marry with the Whyddon family and to inherit a large part of their property, among it the family house itself. They only disappeared as landowners in the parish within the last century.

Metherall was for a short time the possession of Edward, Duke of Somerset. It was granted to him in 1547, when he was Protector of the Realm, during the short reign of the young Edward VI.

Coleshall (later Colehole) was owned by one William Batteshall in 1563; it was later owned by John Laskey, who sold both Hole and Colihole to William Noseworthie, also related to the Whyddons. This was in the early 17th century. Hole House was built in 1668, presumably replacing a medieval farmhouse, probably by the Noseworthies.

The family of Week, who were related to both Knapmans and Northmores, were in possession of Withecombe and Broadwithecombe in 1566, but sold them to Richard Gearde, who in turn sold them to William Knapman. The Weeks had the rights to Padley and Nattadon Commons, which they lost to the Northcotts in 1588.

Frenchbeare was owned by one William Caseley, who sold it to William Newcombe. By the beginning of the 17th century it had become the property of John Hore.

In addition the Rowes were at Holy Street, originally an 11th-century manor. There were freeholdings at Stiniel, Yardworthy, Jurston, Hurston, Thorn, Yeo, and Drewston, and possibly several more of the parish farmhouses were already in existence at this time.

Chagford was a busy Tudor market town. The church and churchyard stood beside the market square. Opposite the church was the Church House and St. Katharine's House, both built at the beginning of this period. The Parsonage House also belonged to this time and was visible from the church. Bellacouch was late medieval or early Tudor and was owned and built by Christopher Coplestone. It was then an L-shaped building, but its lower wing has now disappeared. Besides Bellacouch there was a porch over the church gate, the cross tree stood firmly outside the gate and to the left the lane ran down to Great Week and on to Moretonhampstead; to the right the hill rose to Nattadon, Week Down and Midlecote. Either side of the lane was the glebe land, held by the rector. Opposite the church, Newstrete ran out towards Meldon. Alongside this street were cottages, newly built at the beginning of the Tudor period. The road rose steeply and passed Meldon on its eastern flank, touched the parish boundary at Jurston and followed the boundary to the mines and blowing house at King's Oven.

The Square contained the Stannary Court and was flanked on all sides by the cottages and workshops of the tradesmen of the town.

At the north-west corner of the Market Square a lane descended to Padley Common. Beyond it rose steeply to the ancient house of Waye Barton. Padley Common was common land for the manor, and Waye may have been the site of the demesne of the medieval period. The Prouz family owned Waye Barton from 1345 and were lords of the manor of Shapley, although never of the manor of Chagford.

The oldest part of the present house is Tudor and must date from the time of their ownership.

At Waye Barton the road divided. The King's Way went on to Thorn, Metherall and King's Oven, and from Thorn there was a lane to Teigncombe. The easterly branch from Waye passed round the western flank of Meldon to join the lane to Jurston.

The ancient road to Gidleigh led down to the river at Chagford bridge. Ascending the steep hill on the far side, it forked; the western fork going on to Murchington and Gidleigh, the eastern form to Withecombe and so on to Shilston in Drewsteignton. Travellers coming out of Chagford this way might not cross Chagford bridge, but go on to Holy Street Mill, Leigh bridge, or Teigncombe.

Chagford bridge had been the site of woollen mills in the 13th century, and no doubt still was, although the owner of the enterprise at this time is not recorded. The leat serving the woollen mill remains unchanged and the remnants of a pair of large stone-built buildings at the back of the present kennels may be all that is left of that ancient Devon industry.

At the north edge of Chagford Square a lane went down the hill to the river. On the near bank was the manor and farm of Easton; on the far side of the river the manor of Rushford, reached by Rushford bridge, or by the stepping stones.

In the village itself lived the cottagers and tradesmen. Here was to be found the blacksmith, the plumber (a worker in lead, from the Latin *plumbum*), the harness maker, the tanner, the thatcher, probably many of the tinners, and many of the farm labourers and their families held cottages in the village, with gardens behind.

Communications increased substantially with the coming of the Tudor kings. Central government and trade were both on the increase, and this was bound to bring a demand for highways, inns and bridges, for which the Middle Ages had less need.

The upkeep of the bridges and highways of the parish became the duty of the parish and the churchwarden's accounts give entries for their efforts in this direction. In 1559 they paid 10s. for mending Rushford bridge, and 10s. for timber for Dogmarsh bridge. The bridges were simple granite structures and have been changed little up to the present time. Rushford has only been slightly widened in recent times and, in the 16th century, was probably the same simple granite structure of two arches we see today. Chagford bridge had been in existence since at least 1224, but must have been replaced in the Middle Ages. When Leyland saw it in 1551, it may have been the same three-pointed structure we go over today. Dogmarsh bridge was a handsome granite bridge of three arches, standing a little higher up stream than the present bridge. It was washed away by a flood at the beginning of the 19th century. The present bridge replaced it.

The mending of the roads was dealt with out of the monies collected from the Four Quarters, into which the churchwardens divided the parish. These were Town, Meldon, Teigncombe, and Rushford, and seem to have little in common with the manorial boundaries, and are an example of how the ancient identification of land boundaries had altered.

The primary concern of the parish was agriculture. Little change had occurred in methods since early medieval times, but the pattern of the land had slowly altered

Fig. 4.   Chagford Bridge (from an etching by Samuel Prout)

from the collective farming of the manor, to the family structure that was now the general rule. A large family of several generations could manage a small farm, the larger units would employ labourers and milkmaids, with perhaps a few house servants. The larger houses would have a dairy and a laundry, an orchard, and a cider press.

A moorland parish was a natural habitat for sheep, and the growing wollen industry created added demand for fleeces. Cottagers might have a loom, and a spinning wheel was a common feature of country life. Yarn that was not spun would be knitted. Cattle provided hides for shoes and jerkins, belts, straps and harness.

In addition the tin industry hummed throughout the parish, providing jobs and wealth for many families, great and humble. The metals of the moor must have been utilised within the parish for farm implements, horseshoes, and for weapons.

A market was held in the village weekly; the Stannary Court met twice a year. The weekly market brought all the surplus produce of the parish into the market place and provided not only for additional income to the producer, but was a source of revenue to the owner of the rights. This right was bought by the parish from Master Coplestone in 1564. He continued to receive a yearly rent of 16s. a year from the parishioners, but the profit of the market was hereafter their own.

The dissolution of the monasteries had created a need for poor relief. Collections for the poor were made by the churchwardens from 1558 onwards, and a separate pair of churchwardens took over the job of caring for those in need. These included children, a man whose house had been burnt, and wounded soldiers from the Irish wars.

Chagford had a fine range of skilled craftsmen. They were local craftsmen who built the church and who, at the end of the 15th century, added the tower; who fitted the windows and hung the bells. It was the common practice for young men to be apprenticed to skilled craftsmen for a term of seven years. The following gives a full account of the terms:

> 1580: The 12th day of June 1580 there was agreement made with Augustyn Cayslye of Batheworthye in the parish of Chagford, blacksmith, by William Smyth, Thomas Broke, Thomas Wyll and John Loskye, four men of the parishioners of Chagford and Gregor Fryend and John Norsworthye, ale wardens, with the assent of all the inhabitants of Chagford aforesaid, that the said Augustyn Cayslye shal have one Thomas Lowton, son of one John Lowton late of Chagford, deceased, for the term of seven years. Naming the date thereof to serve with the said Augustyn as apprentice to the art and mystery of a blacksmith during the which term the said Augustyn to teach the said Thomas to the said art or occupation in the best manner that he can and also to find and provide to the said Thomas competent meat, drink and clothing as shall be convenient for apprentices . . . and in the end of the said term to pay or cause to be paid to the said Thomas Lowton the sum of 3s. 4d. of lawful money of England . . . witness Thomas Frenche, Nicholas Podycomb, John Hole and others.

In this way Augustyn Cayslye, Thomas Lowton and the art and mystery of a blacksmith were all provided for and the town content.

The English reformation, with all its accompanying upheavals, touched the spiritual life of the Church. The increasing power and centralisation of the State brought Commissioners from the queen several times between 1558 and 1600. The Four Men, the principal churchwardens, were required to ride to Exeter to report before them. Luckily for Chagford there was an eminent lawyer on hand. In 1530 the churchwardens had paid Master Whyddon 7s. for lawyers' agreements and we may be sure that when any matter of the law arose they would consult John Whyddon, knight and judge, who was also their lord of the manor, on their best course of action.

In 1540 the churchwardens mention a sum of 8d. that they paid at the king's visitation. Henry VIII had been in Exeter the previous year and may have visited his Stannary towns and perhaps his manor of Lydford at the time of his visit.

Despite the agricultural prosperity and trading wealth of these times, the Tudor period also saw intermittent war with France and Spain. In 1546 the churchwardens paid 14s. for cloth and for making coats for the king's needs. The churchwarden's accounts make mention of money paid for arrows and quivers, for uniforms for the soldiers, for a crest, banner and streamer, and for spears. Poor money was given to soldiers wounded in Ireland and we may suppose that the increasing use of Devon's ports for the wars in Ireland and Spain touched Chagford quite closely. Perhaps returning soldiers may have made their way over the moorland highway from Plymouth and passed through Chagford on their way to Exeter. Some of Chagford's men may have fought in these wars.

Colonisation of America had begun—indeed Raleigh himself had been responsible for an attempt to colonise Virginia so that Devon's ports gained an added impetus with the provision of ships and men for the passage across the Atlantic. In the next century a Chagford man was to make history in the colonies.

Queen Elizabeth died in 1603 and James VI of Scotland became James I of England. The *Mayflower* sailed from Plymouth in 1620. The tin industry had begun to decline and the collapse of the Stannary Courthouse in Chagford in the year 1617 occurred at a time when its use was on the point of fading. The woollen industry took over from the tin mining as Chagford's source of wealth, while the gentle bustle of the farmsteads went on unchanged.

A few extracts from the wills of the Prouz family give a little insight into the quality of life in the homes of Chagford's Tudor gentry:

> Will of Margaret Prouz, late wife of John Prouz of Chaggeforde Esq., 20th February 38 Q. Elizabeth (1596).
> To be buried as near as may be to my late husband John Prouz: if I die at Chagford.
> To each of my godchildren, Margaret and Alice Southcott, daughters of Thomas Southcott, Esq., Margaret Prouz, daughter of my son John Prouz, Margaret Pomery daughter of Hugh Pomery Esq., and Philip son of Paschawe Blackmore, one silver spoon or 6 shillings apiece.
> To my godson Robert son of James Cary, one silver salt parcel gilt and 6 silver spoons which I lately bought of John Willes.
> To my grand-daughter Margaret 40 shillings at marriage if she marry with the consent of my executors.
> To Nicholas Prouz, another son of the said John Prouz, one blue long gown, which was my son George Prouz.

> From the Will of George Prouz, dated 1 January, 30 Q. Elizabeth (1558).
> To my mother Mrs. Margaret Prouz, all my goods in my Barton of Waye, also £5 quarterly out of my lease of Ashburton.
> To my sister-in-law Mrs. Phillip Prouz, my best jewel of gold.
> To my cousin George Prouz, son of my brother John Prouz, my reversion which one Osmond Smith now holdeth in parish of Chagford, also all my armour and all my books except my great book called The Bible.
> To my cousin Richard Reynell my book called The Bible . . .

The upheavals of the Reformation had quietened down, the countryside was peaceful and prosperous and then in 1625 Charles I came to the throne. The events of the following 30 years were to give Chagford yet another place in national history.

Tithe Comments on 1593 Return

'The following list of Tithes occurs between the Return of the Market Wardens of October 7th 1593 and that of the Four Men December 23rd 1593.'

> Hereafter ensueth the Customed sute of tyme of Memory used, whereof no Mans Memory ys not to be Contrarie for the payment of certain tithes within the Pysshe of Chagford to the Pson of the said Pshe. Wch Customes were with the assent of the Ancyient Men the XVth day of March in the xxxvjth yere of the Raine of our Sovereine Ladye Queen Elizabeth.
> Imprims. yt hath bin used oute of tyme of memory that no mans mynde is to the contrary.
> For the fawell (foaling) of evye colte to the Pson of the Pshe a pennye.
> Item for evy veiwre (barron cow) two pence.
> Item for evye newed cowe (cow that has just calved) two pence.
> Item for evye culfe two pence.
> Item in consideration of tithing woode to paye evye yere a hewrth penny and no more for all kinds of wood.
> Item for evy spallier (labouring at tin works) a shovell penny.

Item the said Pishners have used out of tyme of memory to bring all there tithing lames when the said Pish to be tithable uppon the Feast of St. Michael's daye to the Churchyard of the said Pishe of Chagford. And the tithe woule whin the said Pish to brought unto the Church Porch of the Pish at the time when the said woule shall be tithable although the Pson or his deptie ne not there yt is sufficyent tender. Likewise they have used to bringe home the tithing waxe and honnye to the Psonage of Chagford according to their consyence.

Item oute of tyme of memory the Pson of the said Pishe oughte to yelde a feaste to the seid pisheners on Tuesday in Easter weeke or allow xxvjs viijd for the same at the election of the said Prnheners.

Item a gardyn penye so called for all fruits saving corn.

Chapter Seven

THE WHYDDON FAMILY

TUDOR TIMES in England were remarkable for the changes in social status that so many families underwent. The feudal barons and nobility lost their position in favour of a new group of influential persons, originally merchants, clerks or yeoman farmers, who owed their rise in position partly to the Crown's fear of the feudal barons, but also because increased commerce, industry and technology made merchants, seamen and lawyers of greater value to the Crown in the days of America and the colonies.

Devon was particularly favoured in this respect, for her seaports produced the families of Grenville, Raleigh, Drake and Hawkins, Queen Elizabeth's most favoured seamen; while any number of intelligent young men, receiving an education in the clergy's grammar schools, would go on to Oxford or Cambridge, or to the Inns of Court in London. Here they would receive a legal education that would stand them in good stead for the rest of their lives.

In this way, during Tudor times, an old Devon family, residents of Chagford, produced a Justice of the King's Bench, Sir John Whyddon, and in so doing, became, however briefly, a family of national repute.

The Whyddon family were probably of British origin, rather than either Norman or Saxon. There is no record of their being either knights or esquires in the Plantagenet era, yet sometime around the end of the 13th century a young man named Whyddon married a daughter and heiress of the family of de Chagford. This Whyddon, the first of whom we have any information, must have been a merchant of some kind and may have come from Exeter, or possibly he was a yeoman farmer of good character and status, otherwise he would never have been in a position to marry a daughter of the lord of the manor. She must have brought him some wealth and perhaps land, but the manor went to the Wibbery family and only became the possession of the Whyddons two centuries later, when the feudal system had lost its hold.

However, Mr. Whyddon and his de Chagford bride must have prospered, for their son, Henry Whyddon, married Jane, daughter and heiress of Wray of London. In the 14th century such a marriage could never have been arranged without contacts in the capital, and lends further weight to the suggestion that the Whyddons were merchants in late medieval times, or possibly already involved in the legal profession, though this seems less likely.

Henry and Jane, apparently residents of Chagford, had a son, Roger Whyddon, whose son, in turn, married Margaret, daughter of Richard Wykes of Coketry in Devon. His name was Simon and he and his wife were also residents of Chagford. Their son,

John Whyddon of Chagford, married Joan Alford and gave her husband a son, also John, who married a Miss Rugg, an old Chagford family, whose name occurs frequently in the churchwarden's accounts.

It was their son, also John, who was to make the family fortune and achieve notoriety as a judge under three different sovereigns. Born at the beginning of the 16th century, John Whyddon was educated in Devon, possibly at the church grammar school in Exeter. He then went to study law at the Inner Temple and was called to the bar. In 1529 he became Autumn Reader of the Middle Temple and Lent Reader the following year. Seven years later he was Double Reader, and in 1539 Treasurer of the Inner Temple. In the last year of Henry VIII's reign he was made serjeant-at-law with seven others, an appointment confirmed by Edward VI when Henry VIII died. A dinner was given for the newly-created serjeants-at-law after the ceremony of which Sir W. Dugdale (*Orig. Jurid.*) gives this account: 'The solemnity being over in Westminster Hall, the said lord chancellour, and other lords and judges, came that day to dinner at Lincoln's Inn; and thither came also to dinner my Lord Mayor of London, Sir John Gresham, with certain aldermen, and the sheriffs of the city, and some other men of worship, which were bidden to the feast; where they were all honourably received; tho' their dinner was not epicurious, nor very sumptuous, but yet moderately, discreetly, and sufficiently order'd, with a wise temperance, without great excess or superfluity, as it was most convenient, and to learned lawyers and sober and expert counsellours was most decent and requisite'.

Six years later, in 1552, Mr. Whyddon was made a Judge of the King's Bench under Queen Mary and knighted the following year. He was reputedly the first judge to ride to Westminster Hall on a horse, since before that time the judges rode on mules. Sir John Whyddon was sent to the north of England to try those who, under Thomas Stafford, had rebelled against the queen and taken the castle of Scarborow in Yorkshire. This job was considered so dangerous that Judge Whyddon sat at the bench in armour, and was given the commission of general in case he needed to take arms against the rebels. For this service to the queen he was given an addition to his coat of arms; a black swan, sitting in a crown, with a golden bill and the motto 'Rara avis in terris, nigrog; simillima Cygno'.

When Queen Elizabeth came to the throne, Judge Whyddon was confirmed in his position, in which he remained throughout the rest of his life, so that at his death in 1575 he had served as a serjeant-at-law for 46 years and as a judge for 22 years. He had served under three very different sovereigns. He was described as 'a man of an high stomach, and well-read in the laws of the land'.

He married twice; first to Anne Hollis, daughter of Sir William Hollis, Kt., by whom he had one daughter, Joan, who married John Ashley of London, Esq.; second, to Elizabeth, daughter and heiress of William Shilston, Esq., by whom he had six sons and seven daughters.

Sir John Whyddon was a tin-owner and this may have contributed to the wealth of the family in late medieval and Tudor times. At his death he was also a considerable land-owner, possessing the manors of Chagford and Teigncombe, the lease of the manor of North Bovey, lands called Oldich in South Tawton, a lease of lands called Padlie, Langland, Brodeland, and Hayelands in Chagford. He had also bought the manor with advowson of Chagford, and, having originally rented the Church House, he had, it seems, now bought it.

Sir John Whyddon was buried to the north of the altar in Chagford church, where a fine Renaissance tomb bears the inscription: 'Here lieth Sir John Whyddon, Kt., one of the Justices of the King's Bench, who ended this life the 27th January 1575'.

Sir John Whyddon's property was divided between his six sons. The eldest, William, married twice, but had no children, and the second son, Edward, became the judge's chief heir. His third son, Oliver, was Archdeacon of Totnes and his father's executor. To him went the judge's house, now the *Three Crowns*. Oliver Whyddon studied at Exeter College, to which he was admitted in May 1563. He became an M.A., and afterwards a Fellow of the College. Later he became rector of Yoxhall and Archdeacon of Totnes. After his death the family house passed to his brother, Francis, the fourth son of Sir John Whyddon.

Meanwhile, the second son, Edward, married one Elizabeth, daughter of William Chudleigh and widow of James Coffin. By this lady he had a son and heir, John Whyddon, also of Chagford. John was knighted at the coronation of King James in 1603, and he was lord of the manor of Chagford and patron of the living. At his death he owned the manors of Shapley and Clifford Cully, together with land in 24 Devon parishes, and five Cornish ones. His wife was Blanch, daughter of Roger Ashford, and by her he had three sons and four daughters.

Sir John Whyddon's heir was his eldest son, William, but he died before his father and the inheritance went to Roger Whyddon, the second son. Roger Whyddon was born in about 1602 and lived in South Tawton. Although he represented the senior branch of the family it appears that much of the Chagford land had gone to his cousin, Oliver, son of Francis, fourth son of the judge.

Roger Whyddon's will shows much of his land made over to others in payment of debts. He seems to have had only one daughter, Elizabeth, to whom he left, beside other things, 'my Topas Juell &c. & my needlework carpet and cushion with Waddam's arms which are at Mr. Parr's, Minister of St. George Clist near Apsome, also my Tin works of Tinmarsh, Smalebrook and Natbrooke and my tin works within the Stannaries of Chagford, Lydford, Tavistock, Plympton and Ashburton'.

Both Roger's brothers had died young and without children, so that Roger Whyddon's property was left to his only daughter. The property had decreased. In 1637 he had sold the advowson of the living of Chagford to William Hayter, rector of Throwleigh and thereby separated it from the lordship of the manor for the first time. His father, Sir John Whyddon, had left many of his large number of properties made over to others in payment of debts, and this gradual dwindling of properties seems to have continued with Roger.

With the death of Roger in 1645, the eldest branch of the family went into the female line.

Roger's cousin, Oliver, who was the owner of the lands at Easton, lived at Woodhouse in Sidbury, and married Margaret, daughter of William Crymes and widow of Arthur Coplestone. She became his heiress and thereafter their son, Rowland Whyddon, was heir, and inherited both Woodhouse and the lands at Easton in Chagford. Rowland was a J.P. under the Commonwealth, and married a Miss Frances

Coplestone, by whom he had five children. Rowland was probably the builder of Whyddon House, which bears, above the front door, the date 1649. The family had held land in Easton since the time of the Judge and may have lived at an older house in that hamlet, perhaps Easton Court, now an hotel.

Whyddon House was built in the year that Charles I was beheaded, and Rowland must have been a good friend of the Commonwealth to have been in a position to build himself a new house at that time. It is a tall square country house at the base of the Teign Gorge. Above it the steep slopes of the deer park, that was created for the house, rise to over 800 feet. The house is enclosed on two sides by steep slopes and high ground, but to the east and west, parkland, now agricultural, gives it a clear view. Quite unlike any neighbouring house of its size, it still contains some of the dark oak panelling and great fireplaces that give it its characteristically 17th-century flavour.

It was Rowland's sister, Mary, who became a legend in Chagford in the saddest circumstances. Tradition says that Mary Whyddon was shot by a jealous lover, at the entrance to the *Three Crowns,* returning from her wedding.

A stone slab set into the floor of the church in Chagford, close to the altar, bears this inscription:

> Mary Whyddon, daughter of Oliver Whyddon, who died in 1641.
> Reader wouldst know who here is laid
> Behold a matron yet a maid.
> A modest look, a pious heart,
> A Mary for the better part.
> But dry thine eyes, why wilt thou weep,
> Such damselles doe not die, but sleep.

In her will which bears neither date nor place, she leaves money to her brothers and sisters, to the poor of Chagford, and the labourers of the parish, to her godchildren and two of her cousins, and a gold ring to her mother. Nothing else is known about her, but we might speculate that her story was the inspiration for R. D. Blackmore's *Lorna Doone,* for the legend of her death has come down by word of mouth in Chagford for generations and might easily have carried as far as Exmoor.

One other member of the family from this period deserves special mention. In 1622 Ichabod Whyddon sailed from Portsmouth to Portsmouth, New Hampshire in the New World, and there began a new branch of the family, whose descendants are alive today, both in Canada and the United States. Members of the American family are still in touch with Chagford, and Mrs. Whyddon Wilson of Portland, Oregon, has sent much in the way of useful information about this branch of the family and pictures of the family christening robe, which show details of the fine lacework. If the Chagford branch of the family went into a decline and slowly disappeared from the parish, another branch were vigorously pioneering the New World.

Legend says that stones from the chapel at Great Week were taken to Whyddon House to repair the garden walls and that this brought bad luck to the family and led to their decline. Perhaps this is true. The eldest branch went into the female line with the death of Roger Whyddon in 1646, and the younger branch, after a phase of inter-marriage by cousins, also disappeared. Whyddons were living in Exeter at least throughout the 17th century, and one Daniel Whyddon was among those who rode on Uncle Tom Cobley's horse to Widecombe Fair.

The last of the family to live in this area may well have been the rector of Lustleigh in the middle of the 19th century, whose brother left a series of charming love letters behind. Copies of these we still have and are included below. Written to a Mrs. Caroline Hicks, it appears that Mr. Whyddon is about to give up his condition of 'solitary philosopher' to marry a charming widow.

After this the story dies away and Whyddon House became the property of the Northmore family. They sold it to the Seymours and by marriage it became owned by the Baileys, until 1921, when Mr. Drew bought the entire property, along with the adjoining land in Drewsteignton parish, on which he built Drogo Castle.

One of the last of the Whyddons of our area, Oliver Whyddon of Moretonhampstead, son of Rowland Whyddon, died in 1724. In his will he left his money and goods in his house to his wife, and his law books to his grandchidren, who were to be brought up to practise the law. This is one last example of that particular strain in the family which made their fortunes and yet never held them, but which ran through many generations, giving them their intelligence and their values, and which is to some extent typical of Devon families of that day.

Lustleigh Rectory
Wednesday
10 oclock p.m. 7th sept 1836

I promised you my dearest Caroline a letter by Friday morning's post but how I shall succeed I know not. If our journey on Monday was attended by a chapter of accidents I may truly say that my wanderings today are strictly in unison with the events of that day. I arrived at Newton at ½ past five and had to try my patience for more than an hour en attendant the Mail. Could I but have known this! dearest! Imagine my finding the Mail as I had anticipated full inside and out. What was to be done? To remain in Newton was to me quite out of the question, so I ordered a Fly at 7 so away I started for my Brother's where I arrived at 9 and had the very great satisfaction of learning that the reverend gent and his wife left Lustleigh for Plymouth about 8 hours previously to return on Friday next. Having cheered the end of disappointment with a cup of refreshing tea I thought I might as well turn all these little contre-temps to the advantage of someone (and for whom so readily as Gyp?) and the result is that I am scribbling to you in order if possible to put you in possession of a few lines by tomorrow's post from somewhere but whether from Ashburton or Plymouth I know not. I have two chances tomorrow by Coach and by the Mail, but both will arrive in Plymouth after 4 in the afternoon. I know not that I can enter on any new subject on which to write you having so lately seen you but if it be any satisfaction to you to see my declaration when you cannot hear them this bears her testimony my dearest girl that I love you sincerely too. Does my last affiliation offend you? If I can continue to send you a line with your boxes possibly under the directions nailed down I will—I am not a little tired dearest from this evening's excursion and therefore I know you will not expect to see a longer letter than this, expecially when you know that I purpose riding over at 7 tomorrow morning to North Bovey to breakfast with Capt. Britten to return here and hence to Ashburton to get home if possible by Coach or Mail. God bless you and protect you. With love to Mamma. Believe me,
                    Yours
                              J.W.

I have opened this dear Cary to say that I arrived here at 5 after riding on horseback 15 miles, as wet as a shag. But here I am. God bless you dear. I am in hopes that you will receive this tomorrow morning. Your sincere J.W.

Wednesday evening
15 March 1837

Once more I have to address my sweet Cary in accord with her wishes and my desire. I turned my back rather unwillingly on Teignmouth on Tuesday morning at the appointed hour and marched away to Newton in true sportsmanlike manner where I arrive quite in time to be conveyed to Plymouth Old Town. This is too much matter of fact with me to need my communication but as my dear Gyps commands in this point I have made a merit of accepting by and bye however when you cannot turn one to the right about I shall not be a complainant. I promise you my dear girl that you are still improving in health if you are improving in that respect in the same ratio that my affection for you is increasing you bid fair to be quoted as a paragon of health and good looks. Heaven protect you and watch over you my fond good Cary. How ardently do I hope that the future may follow out the dream of the present and the relying with sincerity of happiness of the present moment no act or inadvertency of our own may chase it from our grasp.

Chapter Eight

ENDACOTT OF NEW ENGLAND

THE DISCOVERY of the New World and its possibilities affected the life of Devon by virtue of its seaports and its seafaring families, but it touched Chagford closely in the early 17th century, when it became the destination of English Puritans looking for a better world.

The Endacott family had been prominent members of the parish for over a century when one of their sons came under the influence of a Dorset clergyman, the Rev. John White of Dorchester, who was a great Puritan of his day. The philosophy and teaching of this gentleman, along with the temper of the times, was enough to encourage John Endacott to leave his native Chagford for North America, where he became the first governor of the Massachusetts Bay settlement, soon to become the first state in the Union.

The Endacott family took their name from the estate of Endicott, part of the manor of Itton in South Tawton. The earliest version of the name is probably Yondecott—or yonder cote, meaning the further homestead. The family and the homestead had the same name in 1327, for Johannes de Yondecote was assessed for Lay Subsidy in the sum of tenpence. In 1488 the family also acquired the property of Bittbeare in Winkleigh parish.

In 1528 John Endecote acquired lands in the manor of Middlecott in the parish of Chagford. This land contained a tinworks and may have been acquired partly for that reason, for the Endacott family were already involved in the tin industry. Other branches of the family in Throwleigh, Drewsteignton and Moretonhampstead also owned tinworks on their properties.

John Endecote of Middlecott had two sons, Henry and John. The younger John was a churchwarden in Chagford on several occasions, a tin-owner, and seems to have held land at Waye towards the end of his life.

The elder son, Henry, inherited his father's land at Middlecott and added the farm of Drewston to his property in the 1530s. This was one of the outliers of the manor of Middlecott. One of Henry's daughters married into the Knapman family, becoming the bride of Edward Knapman, son of William Knapman, and his wife Alice (née Hore). Edward's brother, incidentally, had married Ann Whyddon, daughter of Sir John Whyddon, the judge.

Henry Endacott had three sons and it was to the eldest, John, that the property of Drewston, with the land in Middlecott, passed at the death of his father in 1585. John lived to the age of 94, and by his wife, Johane, had four sons and one daughter. He lived at Drewston and had additional properties in Moretonhampstead and Drewsteignton.

63

His eldest son, Thomas, married an heiress from Stoke-in-Teignhead named Alice Westlake. It was this couple who were the parents of John Endacott, Governor of Massachusetts. Alice had one other son, Gregory, but he appears to have been a child of a previous marriage. Thomas and Alice also had one daughter.

John Endacott, son of Thomas, must have come under Puritan influence early in his life, apparently living for some time in the neighbourhood of Dorchester, where the Rev. John White held the living of Holy Trinity. John fought for the Protestant religion in the Low Countries, against the Spaniards, and it was after his return from that war that he married his first wife, Anna Gower. Being the eldest male, heir to the family, he must have already been in possession of some wealth in 1628, when he joined with five other wealthy Puritans in buying from the Plymouth Council a grant for the settlement of the Massachusetts Bay, on the eastern seaboard of North America.

On 20 June 1628 he sailed from Weymouth, with his wife, in the ship *Abigail*, and arrived in Naumkeag, New England, on 6 September in the same year. Naumkeag is on the northern side of Massachusetts Bay and is now called Salem. The *Mayflower* had arrived on this same bleak coast only eight years previously with a band of 102 Puritan pilgrims. The voyage of John Endacott in the *Abigail* was the beginning of a wave of emigrations from England to the north east coast of North America. What is now the important and sophisticated city of Boston was then a wild coast with harsh winters and wild indigenous people.

In 1629, the year after his landing, John Endacott was governor of London's plantation in Massachusetts Bay and leader of the earliest settlers in the area. In 1630 he was replaced by Governor Winthrop, but he became Deputy Governor of Massachusetts in 1641 and Governor in 1644. He held a number of offices, whose variety of names reflect the changing conditions of the colony in which he now lived. It is fair to say that he was the chief office holder of his time in New England and he was Governor of Massachusetts for the major part of his life there. The year after his arrival in New England his wife, Anna, died. In August of the following year he re-married, this time to a lady named Elizabeth Gibson, who probably came from England in the party of Governor Winthrop. Of their family, we know that they had at least two sons. In 1655 the Endacotts moved from their Orchard Farm to the town and seaport of Boston and it was here that John Endacott was buried at his death in March 1665.

That he was a stern Puritan is certain. He is recorded as being 'earnest, zealous and courageous', yet just in his dealings with the Indians. But it was part of his earnest endeavour to convert them to Christianity. In 1651 he wrote to the President of the Corporation for Propogating the Gospel among the Indians in New England. One of the results of his efforts was that Chagford raised money for this fund in the New World. Among the parish papers is a list of those members of the parish subscribing to the Propogation of the Gospel among the Indians of the New World. John Endacott retained his connections with his native parish and his family; despite the fact that he had been largely disinherited by his grandfather as a result of his religious beliefs and the road that they had led him to follow.

In 1636 John Endacott brought a suit in Chancery against his uncle Robert Endacott, his grandmother, Johane Endacott, and their co-executor, Henry Hooper of Chagford. He contested the will of his grandfather, John Endacott, who had died the previous year, leaving his grandson disinherited. The case was proved by the executors in favour of Robert and Johane, and John Endacott let the matter drop. In any case property in Chagford would have been of little value to him in his life in the New World, and communication between the two continents was, at that time, too scant to make a further legal battle feasible.

For a glimpse of the life that John Endacott led in New England and the character that he was, I quote from *The Founders: Portraits of Persons Born Abroad who came to the Colonies in North America Before the Year 1701*, by Charles Knowles Bolton.

> Governor John Endecott was born about 1588, probably at or near Chagford in Devon, a quaint village six or eight miles southeast of Okehampton. The Endecotts had been engaged in the mining of tin in this neighbourhood for a century or more. With five other 'religious persons' he purchased, 19 March 1628, a patent of the Massachusetts Bay. Matthew Cradock and Roger Ludlow secured rights immediately, and Endecott, being related to the former through Ann, his wife, was sent out in June to Naumkeag, later Salem. He showed himself 'earnest, zealous and courageous'; he was just in dealing with the Indians, but was curiously impatient with some of his neighbours, with those, for example, who used tobacco or allowed their hair to go uncut. He was 'of so tender a conscience' in religious matters that he allowed three Quakers to be executed, and others to be flogged, while he was Governor, a policy which brought protests from men like Vane, Peter and Saltonstall. And yet he himself protested against harsh treatment of Roger Williams, and was forced to apologise for this patience with a friend in error.
>
> Endecott was the chief office holder of his time in New England: he was assistant in 1628/9, 1630–34, 1636–40, 1645–48; deputy Governor in 1641–43, 1650, 1654; Governor of London's plantation in the Massachusetts Bay, 30 April 1629–12th June 1630; Governor of Massachusetts in 1644, 1649, 1651–53, 1655–64; major general in 1645–48; commissioner of the United Colonies in 1646–48 and President in 1658. He had moved from his 'Orchard Farm' to Boston in 1655.

The Governor strove valiantly to save the Massachusetts Bay charter during the last two or three years of his life, but powerful influences were against him. His opposition to the English church service, and his attitude towards the regicides, had undermined his reputation in London, and Sir William Morrice, Secretary of State, wrote to the General Court of Endacott's disaffection and the King's discontent. While trouble was thus brewing the Governor died, 15 March 1665, aged 77, and was buried 'with great honour and ceremony' in the Granary Burying Ground at Boston. By his first wife, Ann Gower, it is supposed he had no children; by his second, Mrs. Elizabeth (Cogan) Gibson, of Cambridge, England, whom he married 18th August 1630, he had two sons, John and Zerubbabel.

Strong emotion led Endacott to mutilate the English flag in order to destroy the 'popish' cross of St. George, but of this incident Winthrop wrote:

> The only difference between him and others was, he manifested his opinions by his acts, while they, with more prudence and safety, retained theirs in secret.

He could give as one reason for the blowing-up of 21 barrels of powder on a ship, 'God's wrath, because the Captain 'read the booke of common prayer so often over that some of the company said hee had worne that threedbare': yet he could, in beautiful and heartfelt language, commit his sick friend 'into the armes of our deare and loving Father, the God of all our consolation, health and salvation'.

John Endacott's family flourished in the United States, and today we are visited by Don Endicott, Sr., one of the direct descendants of the governor in the eleventh generation, who has volunteered useful information about his ancestor. It is intriguing to know that this gentleman lives in California and, in his work as an aeronautical engineer, he completed the design and development work on the Saturn S5 stage used to get the astronauts to the moon on the Apollo Moonshot. Little could John Endacott, leaving Chagford to sail to the New World in 1628, have imagined that his descendants would have a hand in that far longer voyage of the 20th century.

Chapter Nine

THE CIVIL WAR AND THE DEATH OF A POET

THE EARLY YEARS of Charles I's reign were not easy ones for Devon. The wars with Spain and France not only damaged the woollen industry, which relied on French markets, but also found returning armies of plague-infested soldiers billeted for months at a time, in Plymouth primarily, but also in Exeter and Okehampton. These towns had to provide for the soldiers out of their own funds, while the troops caused civil disturbance and spread disease. The king taxed his country heavily to pay for his foreign wars and the landed gentry were especially hard hit by the king's enforced loans.

Piracy in the Channel, heavy levies of 'ship-money' from Devon to provide ships to combat the piracy, Irish vagrants fleeing the unrest of their own country, over-population despite the plague, and the difficulties of the woollen industry, all contributed to dissatisfaction with the young king and his advisers.

The continuing problems of religious dissension were felt all over England. The tendency of Charles I towards high church friends and his marriage to a Catholic queen were in sharp contradiction to the growing number of Puritans, who were noticeably present in the south-west.

The country folk of Devon, and of Chagford in particular, had survived the religious upheavals of the Tudor period by a general acceptance of each change as it came and by a certain rural compromise that was, in essence, the basis of the Church of England.

Although Chagford may have felt the effects of the decline in the market for 'Devon kersey', for Chagford had its fair share of sheep farmers and spinning, although the heavy taxes and the terror of plague may have disturbed their peaceful days; in those days loyalty to the king was a requisite of stability in everyone's lives and it died hard in them.

Yet parliament was the basis of English freedom and that freedom was being curtailed. Thus Chagford, like the rest of Devon, must have viewed the beginnings of civil war with disquiet and confusion. Natural loyalties were divided and helpful information scarce. Already in 1628, John Endacott of Drewston had followed his Puritan ideals to the New World, and we may suppose that Chagford had its tinge of Puritanism and its fear of popery creeping into the Court. The taking of sides really rested with the gentry. It was they who were J.P.s, who were Deputy-Lieutenants of Devon and who represented the county in parliament. It was they who owned estates where the armies could be gathered and billeted.

Chagford has traditionally been considered a royalist stronghold, and it is probably the case that the remnants of the tin industry and the tinners would consider the king and the Prince of Wales their natural and only overlord. Although the tin industry had begun its decline some time before and the Stannary Courthouse had collapsed in 1617, the town still contained many of the principal tin-owning families of the area and must have identified itself in that way. The Prince of Wales, in his role as Duke of Cornwall, was the Prince of the Stannaries and it was to him that the tinners held themselves responsible.

The farming population, always a conservative element in the community, must have followed the king, for there was no reason for their deserting their traditional loyalty to the sovereign, who was also the supreme head of the Church of England.

On the other hand those employed by the woollen trade might be more inclined to support parliament, for it was the ill-advised actions of the young king which had endangered the prosperity of that industry. This accounts for Moretonhampstead's traditional role as roundhead, for Moreton was a woollen town.

If the parish was naturally more inclined towards the king than towards parliament, it was not necessarily the case that the landed gentry felt the same way. The Monke family were strongly royalist, but they no longer had any influence in Chagford, for Rushford had come to the Hores. Despite the Church of England tradition of the Endacotts, one of their sons had become a whole-hearted Puritan and there may have been others in the family who felt the same.

Family solidarity, so strong in a small inter-marrying community, was heavily split at this time. John Endacott's mother was a Knapman, the Knapmans and the Hores were related to the Whyddons, the Whyddons to the Chudleighs and the Ashfords, yet we cannot suppose that all these families came out in support of the same side.

However, in 1642, when war became inevitable and both king and parliament began to muster their armies, the leading family in Chagford was the Whyddons. Roger Whyddon had inherited his father's estate in 1633, and although his cousin, Rowland, held Whyddon Park, Roger had the *Three Crowns* and the lordship of the manor. In 1637 he had sold the advowson to William Hayter, but he was still the head of the most distinguished of the parish's families.

Roger Whyddon was not resident at Chagford at the outbreak of the civil war, but his cousin Rowland may have lived there at the time. It seems likely that Rowland was a parliamentarian, for he later became a J.P. under the Commonwealth. Also, his uncle, Francis, rector of Moretonhampstead, retained that living in a parliamentarian town throughout the civil war and the Commonwealth; while his son, Francis, Rowland's cousin, was later ejected from the living at Totnes, for noncomformity. There was certainly a streak of Puritanism in the family.

Both Rowland and Roger Whyddon had been brought up in a legal tradition and they may have felt their loyalties deeply divided, for the legal profession owes its loyalties both to the rule of law as executed by parliament, and to their sovereign, whom they serve. Roger's father had been knighted at the coronation of King James, and in any case, the most illustrious of their ancestors, Sir John Whyddon, had been a judge of the King's Bench under two sovereigns, both of whom he had served well.

In all probability, as the armies mustered and England began to take sides, Chagford held its breath and hoped they would not have to become involved. The cities tended to support parliament, Plymouth held out for that side throughout the sieges of the war; but Cornwall was almost wholly royalist and it was a feature of the king's plans to consolidate that strength by making Devon his own.

The king's army in Cornwall was led by Sir Ralph Hopton, who took his forces through Devon in the autumn of 1642, to join the royalists in Cornwall. They captured Tavistock and laid siege to Exeter, but failed to take it and were forced to withdraw to Plympton. They then turned their attention to Plymouth and laid siege to that city. From Plympton they were on surer ground, for the South Hams area was predominantly royalist, and in November of 1642 supporters of the king were mustered at Modbury. Sir John Berkeley and Colonel Ashburnham of the royalist forces were sent out from Plympton to guard the approaches to Modbury, but the Plymouth parliamentarians arrived first and scattered the royalists.

After this the king's supporters moved to Totnes, causing local distress since the town was forced to billet them and the army was liable to forage and pillage without check. After another unsuccessful siege of Exeter the royalists withdrew to Cornwall.

In January 1643 General Stamford, with his parliamentarian forces arrived at Exeter. Meanwhile the Plymouth forces made an unsuccessful incursion into Cornwall, where they suffered a heavy defeat. The Cornish royalists swept back into Devon, one part of the army taking Saltash and laying siege to Plymouth, the smaller part advancing to Okehampton, which they captured.

Up until this point the war had circled around the edges of Dartmoor and although recruiting by the parliamentarians may have absorbed some Chagford men into the war, the armies had remained near the coast. Now, however, Okehampton was occupied by a division of the royalist army.

A body of the parliamentarian forces under Sir John Northcote, an Exeter knight, were now engaged in marching from Barnstaple to Plymouth, and stopped at Chagford, where they were billeted overnight. A force of 500 men, hungry from their long march, must have been a heavy burden for the small parish. If it were the case that Rowland and Roger Whyddon supported parliament, the officers and a fair number of the soldiers might have been billeted at Easton or the Whyddon House, now the *Three Crowns*. This is speculation.

They would have moved on, but at daybreak on 8 February a force of cavalier horse and dragoons, under Sir John Berkeley, surprised them in Chagford, and battle ensued. The royalists were without infantry and apparently only escaped the parliamentarians with difficulty; although royalist reports stated that the parliamentarians fled to Totnes, leaving 140 prisoners and 30 horses laden with provisions.

The fact that Sir John Berkeley's royalist troops were without infantry suggests that he was not in search of the enemy, but may have been searching for supplies for his men at Okehampton. The parliamentarians were certainly unprepared for battle, as at dawn they were probably just beginning their day. Both sides were probably unprepared, and in any case, in war terms it was little more than a skirmish, although in the life of the village it must have seemed nearer an earthquake. Four strangers were buried in Chagford as a result of the fighting, though there is no record that any of Chagford's people lost their lives and they may have remained as uninvolved as possible.

Tragedy. however, befell the royalist forces. Among their number was Sydney Godolphin, a young Cornish gentleman of a family long established in that county. He was the second son of Sir William Godolphin of Godolphin in Cornwall, and Thomasin, daughter of Thomas Sydney of Wrighton, Norfolk. Sydney Godolphin was M.P. for Helston in Cornwall and at the time was aged thirty-three. He was a great friend of Lord Falkland and of the philosopher Hobbes. His commander-in-chief wrote that 'he was as absolute a piece of virtue as ever our Nation bred'.

During the course of the fighting, this young gentleman was shot by a musket and killed. Tradition says that he died in the porch of the *Three Crowns*, which his spirit is said to haunt. It could be that the officers were billeted in this building with the Whyddons and as a consequence this is where much of the fighting took place.

Clarendon's *History* describes the event as follows:

> In these necessary and brisk expeditions, falling upon Chagford (a little town in the south of Devon) before day, the King lost Sidney Godolphin, a young gentleman of incomparable parts; who, being of a constitution and education more delicate, and unacquainted with contentions, upon his observation of the wickedness of those men in the house of commons of which he was a member, out of the pure indignation of his soul and conscience to his country, had with the first engaged himself with that party in the west: and though he thought not fit to take command in a profession he had not willingly chosen, yet as his advice was of great authority with all the commanders, being always one in the council of war, and whose noteable abilities they had still use of in their civil transactions, so he exposed his person to all action, travail, and hazard: and by too forward engaging himself in this last received a mortal shot by a musket a little above the knee,of which he died in the instant; leaving the ignominy of his death upon a place which could never otherwise have had a mention to the world.

Clarendon's view of Chagford testifies to how far it had fallen from its former glory in the days of the Stannary Court. Yet if Sydney Godolphin was to give Chagford fame, it is only fair that I should record here his own fame as a gifted poet, hoping that the two poems quoted here may rest as fair example:

SONG

Or love me lesse, or love me more,
   And play not with my liberty,
Either take all, or all restore,
   Bind mee at least, or set mee free,
Let mee some nobler torture finde
   Than of a doubtful wavering mynd,
Take all my peace, but you betray
   Myne honour too this cruel way.

'Tis true that I have nurst before
   That hope of which I now complaine,
And having little, sought noe more,
   Fearing to meet with your disdaine:
The sparks of favour you did give,
   I gently blew to make them live:
And yet have gained by all this care
   Noe rest in hope, nor in despaire.

I see you weare that pittying smile
   Which you have still vouchsaft my smart,
Content thus cheaply to beguile
   And entertaine an harmlesse hart:
But I noe longer can give way
   To hope, which doth soe little pay;
And yet I dare noe freedome owe
   Whilst you are kind, though but in shew.

Then give me more or give me lesse
   Does not disdaine a mutuall sence,
Or your enpittying beawties dresse,
   In their owne free indifference.
But shew not a severer eye
   Sooner to give mee liberty
For I shall love the very scorne
   Which for my sake you doe put on.

HYMN

Lord when the wise men came from farr,
Led to thy cradle by a Starr,
Then did the shepheards too rejoyce,
Instructed by thy Angells voyce:
Blest were the wisemen in their skill,
And shepheards in their harmlesse will,

Ther is noe merrit in the wise
But love, (the shepeards sacrifice).
Wisemen all ways of knowledge past,
To th'shepheards wonder come at last:
To know, can only wonder breede,
And not to know, is wonders seede.

Wisemen in tracing Natures lawes
Ascend unto the highest cause,
Shepheards with humble fearefulnesse
Walke safely, though their light be lesse:
Though wisemen better know the way
It seems noe honest heart can stray.

A wiseman at the Altar bowes
And offers up his studied vowes
And is received; may not the teares,
Which spring too from a shepheards feares,
And signs upon his fraylty spent,
Though not distinct, be eloquent?

'Tis true, the object sanctifies
All passions which within us rise,
But since noe creature comprehends
The cause of causes, end of ends,
Hee who himselfe vouchsafes to know
Best pleases his creator soe.

Clarendon, in addition, said of Godolphin, that he was 'of so nice and tender a composition, that a little rayne or winde would disorder him . . . when he ridd abroad with those in whose company he most delighted, if the winde chanced to be in his face, he would (after a little pleasant murmuringe) suddaynely turne his horse, and go home'.

Perhaps it was no wonder that so gentle a young poet should have little experience of war and fighting and, being too eager to face the enemy, fall an easy prey to their muskets.

*   *   *   *   *

The young poet's body was removed to Okehampton by Sir John Berkeley and he was buried there two days later on 10 February 1643.

Okehampton was to see a great deal of the hardships of war, for the royalists were billeted there from this time until the New Model Army of Cromwell arrived in Devon in the winter of 1645.

Chagford had seen its only battle of the war, but its problems were not over, for the royalist armies that held Devon throughout the following three years were a heavy burden on the county.

By the autumn of 1643 the royalists held all of Devon with the exception of Plymouth. The army in Okehampton was maintained by the town. But it was a feature of the civil war that both sides were short of funds to pay for the upkeep of their soldiers, with the result that the local people were called upon to provide the necessary food and shelter. Different commanders used different methods, billeting their soldiers on the local population, taking heavy assessments from the Hundreds, exacting horses, money and arms from the landowners, or simply failing to make provision for their men, who were forced to raid and pillage in order to provide for themselves.

In addition the commanders might force the local men into their army, while the frightening condition of local law and order made it even more necessary for able-bodied men to remain at home to protect their property and families.

In the summer of 1644 Queen Henrietta Maria arrived in the south west, where her daughter was born. Shortly afterwards the king arrived in Exeter, where he saw his daughter for the first time. The queen stayed two nights in Okehampton on her way to France, and shortly afterwards the king brought his army through Crediton and Bow on his way to Cornwall, where he defeated General Essex's remaining parliamentarian forces.

The south west now became the focus of the king's war efforts, until the defeat of his armies at Naseby in June 1645 left the parliamentarian army in eastern England free to move to the south west.

In July a gathering of the local population in Crediton proposed to the Commissioners of Devon that if they might have Sir Richard Grenville as their commander and if no attempt was made to take them outside Devon without their consent, they would provide themselves with arms and munitions at their own expense to fight the parliamentarian army. The Commissioners would not give them Sir Richard Grenville as commander, and the proposal came to nothing, but the people of Chagford may have been represented at the meeting, and, despite the misery of the previous years, still been prepared to fight for the king.

The New Model Army reached the south west in the autumn of 1645 and Cromwell defeated the royalists at Bovey Tracey in January 1646. From this time on the parliamentarians slowly regained the south west. In February they were at Crediton, Great Torrington was captured in the same month, Cornwall was subdued, Plymouth liberated, and finally Exeter fell into parliament's hands. There must have been skirmishing along the River Teign during this period, for the Fulfords, who owned a large estate at Dunsford, were staunchly royalist and pockets of cavaliers were to be found by the enemy hidden in many folds of the countryside. It was probably during the advance of Fairfax and Cromwell that the cavalier lost his life in the woods near Fingle Bridge. Although he might have been a straggler from the fighting in 1643, it is perhaps more likely that he and perhaps one or two others were ambushed in the Gorge during the fighting at Dunsford and that he was killed there. His grave bears no name or date, just a simple cross and is known as the Cavalier's Grave.

In May of 1646 Charles I surrendered to the Scots and was later handed over to parliament. For Chagford there was a period of peace, albeit an uneasy one. The king was beheaded in 1649 and after four years of confusion Cromwell became Lord Protector in 1653. It was in this period that German Gouldstone was rector of Chagford, for many Church of England parsons lost their livings in the confusion of those years.

With the introduction of Cromwell as Lord Protector in 1653 all Protestants were given a certain tolerance and more normal conditions returned to the Church of England. In 1655 John Coplestone became rector of Chagford, and in 1662, after the restoration of Charles II George Hayter became rector of the parish at the presentation of his own trustees. Peace had returned to the Devon countryside, which was to see no more war until the 20th century.

Chapter Ten

THE HAYTER AND HAMES FAMILIES

THE REVEREND WILLIAM HAYTER was the first member of the family to live in this area. In 1644 he was rector of Throwleigh. He was a member of a Wiltshire family whose home was near Salisbury, some of whose members remain in that part of England to the present time. There is no record of what brought William Hayter to Devon, but in 1637 he had bought the advowson of Chagford from Roger Whyddon and so put down roots that find myself and my sisters settled in Chagford today.

The development of the Chagford living had left the glebe as the property of the patron. When he appointed a rector, the income from the glebe would provide a living for the rector, supplemented by the tithes of the parish. In Chagford the glebe never reverted to outright ownership by the church, but remained the property of the Hayters. Since every generation of this family provided at least one rector, not only the ownership of the property, but also the income remained in their hands.

William Hayter was born in 1599 and went to Exeter College, Oxford, where he gained his M.A. He must have come to Devon during the reign of Charles I, and acquired the patronage of Chagford shortly before the outbreak of the Civil War. During the Commonwealth a character known as German Gouldstone was rector of Chagford. The Hayters survived the turmoil of those years, and after Charles II was restored to the throne, William's son, George Hayter, became rector of Chagford. He gained his M.A. from Oriel College, Oxford, in 1661, and took up the living of Chagford the following year. His wife's name was Anne and, in all probability, they occupied the Parsonage House, which stood nearer the church than the present Chagford House and must have been a typical Tudor family house, with oak timbers and central passage. George Hayter's son, also named George, was probably raised here.

The elder George died in 1679 and his wife, Agnes, inherited the advowson. She introduced the next rector, William Reade, archdeacon of Barnstaple. In those days a man might hold several ecclesiastical appointments and leave the holding of services and care of his flock to a curate. If William Reade resided at Barnstaple, this might have been the case in Chagford and the Hayters might have remained at the parsonage undisturbed. In 1701 the younger George came into the living at the appointment of his own Trustees. His wife's name was Grace, and by her he had four sons and five daughters.

The eldest of these sons, Thomas Hayter, was born in 1702. He was educated at Blundell's School, Tiverton, and from there he went to Exeter College, Oxford, where he gained his B.A. in 1724. His father died in 1728 and his trustees held the patronage until he came of age. In 1727 he was an M.A. of Emmanuel College, Cambridge,

73

although he was already, at this time, chaplain to the Archbishop of York, Dr. Blackburne, who apparently had a great affection for the young man. Gossip said that Thomas was the natural son of Blackburne, who had been something of a buccaneer in his youth, but it seems that the two men were simply temperamentally inclined to like each other and that this was the basis of their friendship. From this appointment onwards, Thomas Hayter achieved a succession of honours. In 1730 he was Sub-Dean of York, in 1739 Prebendary of Westminster, and from 1730 until 1751 he held the post of Archdeacon of York. In 1749 he was made Bishop of Norwich, and two years later became tutor to the sons of Frederick, Prince of Wales.

Politics were to cut short his appointment at the Court. Thomas Hayter was a liberal thinker and a friend of the Whigs. His tolerance of dissenters made him no friend to the Tory opposition. After squabbles at the Court he resigned his post as tutor to the princes, one of whom was later to become George III. Thomas's health began to fail and he was subject to attacks of gout, which took him to the waters of Bath, Epsom and Buxton, and to the health resort at Malvern. This did not stop him from accepting, in 1761, the Bishopric of London, becoming also Dean of the Chapel Royal and a Privy Councillor. These appointments were due to the favour of his former pupil, who had become George III in 1760. The new king gave Thomas Hayter an ivory likeness of himself as a gesture of friendship. The bishop only held his new post for one year, dying on 1 January 1762, and being buried at Fulham.

He was described as 'a sensible and well-bred man'. He was scholarly and unemotional, but a liberal in his views. He was a lover of civil and religious liberties, remembered for his excessive sympathy with dissenters and as a result suspected of heterodoxy. A sermon preached by Thomas Hayter, then Bishop of Norwich, before the king in 1755, brings the image of a tolerant, thoughtful man, turning over in his mind the best use of human reason. His tolerance of dissenters, his friendship with the Whigs, who had brought the Hanoverians to the throne to protect England from a Catholic king, and his scholarly approach to his religion, suggest a man who was Protestant by virtue of personal belief and deep reflection rather than by habit or position. He died, unmarried and without issue in 1762. The patronage of the living of Chagford passed to his brother, George.

George Hayer was the elder of the remaining sons of George and Grace. He lived at St. Pancras Lane, London, and was a banker. He became Director of the Bank of England and died on 17 December 1784. Of his children one son, George Garrard, and a daughter, Grace, survived him.

At the death of his father, George Garrard Hayter inherited the advowson of Chagford. He was not thirty-two. Educated at Exeter College, Oxford, he became rector of Compton Bassett in Wiltshire. He remained unmarried and died in 1825 at the age of seventy-three.

His uncle, Joshua Hayter, was meanwhile rector of Chagford. He was the youngest son of George and Grace, their third son, John, having died as a child. Joshua was born in 1718, was educated at Westminster, and became an M.A. of Christ Church, Oxford. He was presented to the living at Chagford in 1741 by his brother, Bishop Thomas Hayter. Joshua married a wife named Frances, who surname is unknown. When she died in 1791 at Chagford, she was buried at St. Sidwell's in Exeter, so perhaps this was her original home.

Joshua and Frances had four sons. The eldest died without issue, and the third son died as a child. The second son, George, was born in 1748 and was an M.A. of Oxford. He became rector of Minden and Feering in Essex, and died without issue in 1829.

The youngest, John, became rector of Chagford in 1779, eight years after the death of his father. The patron at this time was his uncle, George Hayter, the banker, who presented him. The Rev. John Hayter was educated at Eton and became a Fellow of King's College, Cambridge. He was also rector of Hepworth in Suffolk. He was an eminent Greek scholar and, after giving up the living of Chagford in 1810, became chaplain to H.R.H. the Prince Regent, by whom he was employed in unrolling and deciphering the Herculanean manuscripts. Polewhele referred to him as 'our classical friend Hayter'.

He married twice: first Lydia Southmead, daughter of the Rev. J. Southmead of Holy Street, but she died tragically young in 1784 at the age of eighteen; second Elizabeth Baskerville, daughter of Captain Peter Baskerville, R.N., of West Cowes, who bore him six sons and three daughters. After giving up the living he devoted himself to his classical studies. John died six years later in 1816. When John Hayter gave up the living it was taken up by the Rev. John Moore, who was principally non-resident. John's cousin, George Garrard, was at this time patron, but at his death in 1825 the only surviving male representatives of the family were the children of John Hayter. The patronage of the living went to George Garrard's sister, Grace.

Grace Hayter was born in 1756 and baptized at St. Mary le Bowe. In 1788 she married John Hames, of Croydon, Surrey, who belonged to an old Leicestershire family long widespread in that county. He may have been a younger son who had had to seek his fortune elsewhere. He had been married before and already had four sons by his first wife, Jane Greening.

Grace was 33 when she married, which probably explains why she had only two children, a small family in those days. They were both sons, named George and William. George was the elder, went up to Oriel College, Oxford, and was presented to the living of Chagford in 1819 by his uncle, George Garrard. Only a year later he died at the age of 29, in his carriage on the way back from Exeter. He was buried at Chagford.

John Hames had died in 1804, but Grace was still alive. She and her husband had lived at Croydon, where he was settled when they married, and Grace's mother lived with them there after her husband's death, and subsequently died there. Grace may have moved to Chagford at the introduction of her son, George. In any case she died there in 1837 and was buried in the same vault as her eldest son, who had died 17 years before. William took up the living at the death of his brother. The patronage was still in the hands of his uncle, George Garrard, but that gentleman was comfortably settled in Wiltshire. William was educated at Westminster and at Emmanuel College, Cambridge, and became rector of Chagford in 1821. When his uncle died four years later he inherited the advowson through his mother.

The only remaining Hayters were the children of William's great-uncle John. Of the six only one had survived his father and that was George, who was in the army and died a bachelor in Plymouth in 1827.

William Hames, therefore, became the last male descendant of the Hayters. Had these ancestors been simply country rectors, no doubt he would have remained solely a Hames. But Bishop Thomas Hayter and the Rev. John Hayter were still well-remembered figures and he could not drop that inheritance so lightly.

Grace Hames died in 1837, the year that the young Victoria came to the throne. William was already the father of a family. He had married in 1824 Jemima Belinda Perkins, daughter of the Rev. John David Perkins, who was rector of Mamhead, of St. Lawrence, Exeter and of Dawlish, where his daughter wed William Hames. The Rev. J. D. Perkins was chaplain to King George IV and King William IV, and was the eldest son of John Perkins of Ufton Court in Berkshire. Jemima Belinda's mother was a Devon lady, being Bridget Northcote, grand-daughter of Sir Henry Northcote of Pynes.

It was probably William Hames who was responsible for the building of the present Chagford House. The parsonage house was apparently burnt, as was not unusual for houses of timber and thatch, and a new Georgian house built on a slightly different site. The living was a good one and the family prosperous enough to give themselves the benefit of the large light rooms and graceful proportions that belong to the Georgian period. Within the house the literary preoccupations of so many members of the family gave rise to the vast collection of books, classical and religious, that lined the walls of my childhood. The house was probably built in the early years of the 19th century, but was in a style that belonged more to the previous century, for Devon is slow to change its ways and retains fashions and styles long after London has capitulated into a new age. In any case, a parish magazine of 1868 gives a life of one John Collins, by trade a carpenter, who was born in 1776 and in 1800 was the only one in Chagford who could put on a slate roof. He was the principal carpenter in the erection of Chagford rectory (now Chagford House).

Here William and Jemima raised their family. Above the fireplace in the drawing room the portrait of John Hames looked down at them, as they went through those early years of Victoria's reign with their son and daughter. Jemima Hayter Hames was the elder, born at Chagford rectory on 13 August 1825. Her brother Hayter George Hayter Hames, was born there on 26 December the following year. William's property consisted of the advowson, with its house and glebe, some capital invested in stocks and shares, and a property in Hammersmith, with another in Holloway that he inherited from his father. He also rented three houses in Piccadilly from the estate of Her Majesty, and for these three he paid £190 a year. What he did with these properties is not clear, but it may be that he kept them for the use of himself and his family when they visited the capital. His solicitors were in Lincoln's Inn Fields and it may be that he did a certain amount of business in London.

As a country rector and J.P. he ran his church in accordance with the habits of the time and attended the Magistrates Court to sit on the bench. The family bible, in which are recorded the names and dates of himself and his children, was probably used at family prayers, which the household would attend.

His daughter Jemima married John Northmore at Eastbourne in 1863. Her father's property in Hammersmith and Holloway became part of her marriage settlement, while John Northmore bought Cleve from his brother, where it seems the couple lived. Jemima, however, had no children, for she died only six years later in 1869 at Torquay, and she was buried at Chagford.

William was rector of Chagford for 31 years, but gave up the living in 1852 in favour of his son. He also held the living of Ham, in Kent, which he retained to the end of his life in 1859.

Hayter George Hayter Hames was educated at Christ Church, Oxford, and became engaged at the age of 26 to Constance Harriet Colville, daughter of a forceful gentleman named Colonel Sir Charles Colville, of Duffield Hall in Derbyshire. A letter from William Hames to Constance at the time of her engagement survives:

> The Rectory
> Chagford
> Nr. Exeter
> 10 June 1852

My Dear Miss Colville

George's letters to me are very amusing: so full of ardour and affection for his 'dearest Constance'. His enthusiasm reminds me of some of the happiest days of my life some twenty seven years ago. I have always liked his singleness of heart, and am rejoiced to find that he has fixed his heart on one of whom I have such a good opinion, and for whom I hope to cherish the highest regard, and friendship to the end of my life.

I have not been very well of late, or I should have joined Mrs. Hames and Jemima in town. They both express themselves highly delighted (as needs they must be) at the coming event.

I have written Colonel Colville by this post   believe me

> My dear Miss Colville
> Most sincerely yours
> W. Hames

Hayter George was presented to the living of Chagford on 2 August 1852 and married Constance ten days later at St. James's Church, Piccadilly. She brought with her, in her marriage settlement, a substantial interest in various properties elsewhere in England and when the value of these was realised, the money was used to buy the Rushford Estate, comprising Rushford Mill, Rushford Barton, and Rushford Wood, which they acquired in 1856.

William Hames died in 1859 and was buried at Chagford. His widow and his son now presented a new set of glass in the east window of the church in memory of him. It was made by the firm of Beer in Exeter, who had a stained glass works in St. Bartholomew's Yard. Mr. Beer's letter to Hayter George, in which he gives instructions for the preparations for erection, goes on to say: 'The whole of the glass I am glad to say, looks well—the Tracery "will look gay and light". I have not shown the window to any once since you called'.

With the death of his father, Hayter George became the head of the family. He was patron and rector of Chagford for over thirty years and was also a J.P. Constance lacked no enthusiasm in providing for the needs of the parish. Her first child was born at the rectory in the first year after her marriage and named Constance Julia. By the time of her father-in-law's death in 1859 she had borne four daughters and a son; the following year another daughter, Augusta, was born, and in 1865 she gave birth to Beatrice.

This in no way deterred her from her work in Chagford. The year after her marriage she had opened an infants' school, and later in the same year she presented an organ to the church. This gift saw the end of the old string band, which had served the musical needs of the church for as long as anyone cared to remember. The third of her daughters, Kathleen, had died as an infant, and in 1857 she donated the present granite font to the church, removing the previous one of Portland stone, which revealed the more ancient font buried beneath, which was then taken and buried in the rectory garden.

Hayter George and Constance were responsible for a complete change in the interior of the church. In 1853 the pulpit was removed from its position over the central aisle and placed by the southern chancel pillar. In 1857 the plaster and whitewash were removed from the pillars and arches, and the remains of old wall paintings over the arches and coloured stripes around them were found. These were the medieval decorations that had been spoiled in the time of Edward VI. In 1861 Hayter George replaced the old reredos with a new granite one which stands below the east window. In 1865 a full restoration of the church was undertaken. Subscriptions were collected from the parishioners, headed by a gift of £250 from the rector. The old pews, which were high and uncomfortable, were removed, and the church re-seated. The plaster was removed from the walls, revealing the granite. The arrangement of the chancel was altered, and the screens, standing between the side chancels and the north and south aisles were found to be rotten and had to be removed, the central screen having previously been removed. Pictures from that year show scaffolding around the tower, which was presumably repaired. In 1867 a new clock was installed in the tower, by subscription from the parish. It was made by Benson of Exeter. In 1870 the arch to the tower was opened, the gallery removed, and the new organ removed to its position at the north-east corner of the church. Four years later, Hayter George's sister, Jemima Northmore, died, and in her memory painted glass was erected in the west window of the tower.

The rector and his wife did not confine their activities to the church; they were also active in the village. The old Market House that stood in the centre of the Square had fallen into such a state of disrepair that it had acquired the name of 'The Shambles', and this was demolished. In July 1862 Constance Hames laid the north-east corner-stone of the new building that now occupies the centre of the Square. This project appears to be very much the result of her personal efforts. The architect was Mr. Herbert Williams and the contractors were Messrs. W. Stone and T. Ball; the inspiration was probably Constance herself.

Her husband, a man of energy, foresight and determination, turned his attention to the water supply. In 1866 he planned a modern drainage system and brought to Chagford a supply of pure water to replace the old 'Town Lake'. The open drains that had run through the village mercifully disappeared.

In 1869 he formed a gas company which provided gas-light for the village, but when this became expensive he changed his ideas to electricity, so that in 1889 an electricity company was formed, which used the water-power at the site of the old woollen mill to provide light for the houses and streets of Chagford, which became the first place west of London to use electricity for street lighting. He was also responsible for the creation of a library and reading room in the village.

The efforts of this energetic couple gave rise to a series of summer concerts, which were held in the parochial schoolroom. Other concerts and musical evenings, along with readings of poetry and Shakespeare, performances by the Chagford orchestra and band, and a wide variety of entertainments, amused the parishioners and helped to bring distinguished guests to Chagford. This seems to have been a part of the rector's intentions, for Baring-Gould, writing in 1900, says:

> Chagford owes almost everything to a late Rector, who, resolved on pushing the place, invited down magazine editors and professional litterateurs, entertained them, drove them about and was rewarded by articles appearing in journals and serials, belauding Chagford for its salubrious climate, its incomparable scenery, its ready hospitality, its rural sweetness and its archaeological interest. Whither the writers pointed with their pens, thither the public ran, and Chagford was made. It has now every appliance suitable—pure water, electric lighting, a bicycle shop, and doctors to patch broken heads and set broken limbs of those upset from their 'bikes'. Chagford is undoubtedly a picturesque and pleasant spot. It is situated near Dartmoor and is sheltered from the cold and from the rainy drift that comes from the South-west.

Apart from their work in the parish, Hayter George and Constance had to care for their family and to see to the management of their land. There are photographs of the family out in the hay-field, the girls sitting with their mother against the turned hay, while the men pitch-forked it into the high-sided cart. Father and son would ride about the parish, while mothers and daughters would go for a drive in the carriage or trap.

The last of the Hayters, George Hayter, died in Plymouth in 1878, and Hayter George assumed the prefix surname of Hayter, which up to that point had simply been a family name.

In due course the daughters became engaged and married. Constance Julia married Captain Studdy in 1874; Georgina Amelia married Major-General Edmund Holley of Oaklands, Devon, in 1879; Isabel Harriet married twice, first in 1878 to Lieutenant R. Constaple, and second to Edward Milner-Jones, a barrister-at-law, of Valindre, South Wales. In 1890, four years after the death of her father, Augusta Jemima married Major William Addington.

As Hayter George neared the end of his life a problem arose. It was a feature of the advowson that if Colville did not take Holy Orders and one of his sisters married a clergyman, that gentleman would have a right to the living. As things stood that would have meant that Colville, the only son, would have to give up the rectory house to a brother-in-law. Father and son took legal advice from their solicitors about the problem. At last they found a solution. The advowson was strictly under the control of the family trustees and was furthermore a natural concern of the church authorities. In effect, Colville divided the glebe, buying outright and freehold the Chagford rectory and its surrounding land, and selling to the church 52 acres on the other side of the lane to Nattadon. With the money realised by this sale he erected a new rectory house on the 52 acres that he was selling. In this way the family home remained his property, while provision was made for an independent rector. The sale was finally arranged in 1887, after Hayter George had died; the old rectory house was known as Chagford House, the new Victorian building became Chagford Rectory.

Whether Colville knew of his sister's affections, or whether they only became clear rather later, it was as well for him that he was able to take this step. At the death of Hayter George, the living became vacant. Colville did not have a vocation for the church. A new rector was appointed. The choice of the family fell upon a young man named Gerald Ley, who Colville himself described as 'spiritually so far above us all'. A year after taking up the living, which he saw as a grave responsibility having the care of 1,500 souls, Gerald married the youngest daughter of the late rector. This was Beatrice, who, with her husband, came to be loved dearly by the parishioners. Gerald and Beatrice moved into their new rectory and raised a family of six children.

Colville remained at Chagford House with his widowed mother, Constance. She died in 1893, and four years later, at the age of 38, Colville married a young lady called Violet Bradshaw. She was the daughter of Octavius Bradshaw, who rented Powderham Castle from the Devons. This lady, who was my grandmother, was a true Victorian. She ruled her house with a firm hand and was remembered in the village 'for her grace and dignity'. She came from a family of one son and five daughters, with whom she was constantly in touch. A letter from her sister, describing the funeral of Her Majesty, gives an indication of those times.

My dearest Vi.

I am so sorry you did not come to town also Col. to see the procession. It was a wonderful sight, gorgeous in its simplicity. All the soldiers and sailors marching with their arms reversed and at such a slow walk. How cramped their arms must have been. I will show you when I come to you how they marched, it must have been dreadful marching 4 miles like it. Cecil looked very grand and stately on his charger, beautifully turned out. Little Allfrey was very busy trotting up and down seeing after his   . Gilbert Troyte also was in the procession, but we did not make him out. He is off to Africa this week. It was so funny to see the cream coloured horses, with their beautiful harness of red and blue and brass drawing the gun-carriage with the Royal standard placed on and then the coffin which was covered with a beautiful embroidered white satin pall on which rested 3 crowns, a big one and a diamond one and another. Then came the King, on his right the German Emperor and on his left the Duke of Connaught. Then all the other royalties came jumbled up together. I only made out the King of Portugal, the Crown Prince of Germany and the Duke of Saxe-Coburg. They all came so quickly and not in line it was quite hard to see them and their gorgeous uniforms. All the ladies were in closed carriages and very black so we could not distinguish them. All the horses were draped with purple. It was so pretty and yet so curious. They were magnificently done. The seats were going at tremendous prices. We had quite difficulty in getting a seat in the train —it was crammed. There were such lots of soldiers being taken back at the same time. We got home soon after 12 this morning nearly dead. I am glad to say nobody has come in today so I shall be able to retire early to bed. I am hunting tomorrow and have to start early. Am enclosing you the receipt of Goberk, it came to £1.8.-. What train would you like me to come by on Thursday. Am so looking forward to coming to you and will try to remember to bring Dante with me.   Lots of love
                                                    your loving sister
                                                         Leila.

I hope the cheese scoop will arrive in time to bring with me.

Colville managed his land, executed his duties as a Justice of the Peace, and was a keen rider. Many of his letters describe his days in the field or end in haste so that he can set off for the meet. A letter from one of his tenants, quoted here, gives, I hope, a fair indicationof local feeling about him.

> Higher Withecombe
> Chagford
> July 10th 1910.

Dear Sir,

In answer to your letter. It was a great pleasure for me to be able to send my men in to help save your hay, and I am sure I could do ten times has much for you. You have acted such a gentleman to me althrough my 24 years tenancy. As to sending cheque there is nothing to pay you have done more than that for me. Thanking you for all your kindness to me.

> Yours Respectfully
> Charles Jeffery.

Colville and Violet had two sons. The elder, George, was born in July 1898, Noel was born on 24 December 1901. The two boys grew up together and learnt to fish and to ride. A series of governesses taught them their lessons until they were old enough to go to Winchester. Coming home from school for the holidays they would stop at Steps Bridge and try to catch a trout.

Then the war broke out. George was sixteen, Noel was thirteen. Their father was now too old to join the forces and was given the job of buying local horses from farmers and from hunting people to equip the army. He was well suited for this, as riding and horses were one of the passions of his life.

At the age of 18 George left school and went into the 1st Life Guards, serving in France. Noel was too young to join the forces, but after school he went into the air force, first at Cranwell College, which he left with the Sword of Honour, and then as a pilot, becoming stationed in India.

George had meanwhile gone up to Oxford, where he read agriculture at Christ Church, receiving his B.A. in 1921. He then went out to India to join his brother. At the gift of their grandfather, Octavius Bradshaw, they climbed in the Himalayas, where they hunted the mountain game, ibexes and makaws. They climbed Nungapervit and travelled through Nepal into Tibet. This was the last holiday they were to spend together. George returned to England and went into a firm of chartered accountants in order to learn that business. He hunted with the Mid-Devon Hunt, and played polo, which he had seen played in Tibet.

In 1925 Noel was shot down over the north-west frontier of India and killed. He was buried there, and his parents were only to see photographs of his grave. They erected the beautiful chancel screen in the church in his memory. This tragedy broke his father's heart. Colville survived his son by only three years, dying in 1928. The pulpit was then given to the church in his memory.

Mother and elder son were left at Chagford House. George went into Barclays Bank in the same year that his father died, and later became a local director. From that time onwards his life was devoted to his native county.

In 1933 he joined the Devon County Council, became an alderman in 1945 and chairman of Devon County Council in 1955, a post he held for 10 years. From 1939–47 he was Chairman of the Devon War Agricultural Committee; he was active in the Young Farmers Clubs and was a local chairman of the N.F.U. He was chairman of the Devon Agricultural Association. His tremendous efforts for agriculture in Devon earned him the C.B.E. in 1941, and in 1957 he was given a knighthood in the Queen's Birthday Honours List.

At home he had inherited the land his father had owned at Rushford; he added to this during his life, and took a keen interest in every detail of the life of the farm, where he spent his free time. He was also chairman of the Governors of Seale-Hayne Agricultural College and instrumental in setting up the Agricultural College at Bicton. Apart from his work as a banker and his tremendous interest in agriculture, he was asked to take and always accepted a wide variety of official jobs. Among these positions he was a J.P. and a Deputy Lieutenant of Devonshire, a vice-chairman for Devon of Westward Television, Sheriff of Devon in 1943, and President of the Devon County Show in 1966. He was also chairman of the Dartmoor National Park Committee.

Like his forebears, he was a devoted churchman. He was patron of Chagford after the death of his father, presented the rectors and was a churchwarden. He took the keenest interest in the affairs and life of the church, whose teaching was in any case the foundation of his moral code.

The volume of his work was already great when at the age of 51 he met and fell in love with my mother. Her maiden name was Anne Longfield Flower, and she was a great deal younger than him. They were married in London in 1950 and my father took on a new, and what was to become his favourite job, the care of his family.

Where Hayter George's attention had been focused solely on Chagford, his grandson's belonged to the whole county of Devon. As a young man he had hunted a great deal and enjoyed shooting, but the great obsession of his life was fishing. He knew every inch of every one of Devon's rivers and probably most of the fish in them. On summer evenings he would fish for sea-trout in the Teign and would have to be hauled out in the early hours of the morning.

In 1935 he bought the lordship of the manor of Chagford from Mrs. Ellis. During the Second World War he ran the Home Guard in Chagford and was on the board of Chagford school. A corner of his land was turned into a swimming pool for the parish.

My grandmother, Violet Hayter-Hames, died in 1967, at the age of ninety-three. We were not to know then that my father would survive her by only one year. The responsibilities, the long working hours, the endless different bodies requiring his attention, and the effect of frequent official dinners with speeches and toasts on a man who sensitive, nervous and shy was too much. He became almost completely paralysed in 1967 and after a partial recovery that allowed for some fishing, he became paralysed once more and died in October 1968. At this time the patronage passed to my mother, who presented to the living until the patronage was taken out of her hands by the bishop. The old title had returned to the church.

Although his shyness had probably made him something of a stranger to people, I think my father's life was well-known to Chagfordians, and it is probably true that those generations of rectors, working around the parish and presiding over its church, created in my father one of the warmest loves for his home that any man can have. His own words sum him up very well. 'I'm very impatient. But I suppose I am an enthusiast.'

Chapter Eleven

THE QUIET YEARS (1662–1837)

WITH THE END of the Civil War and the restoration of Charles II to his throne, political upheaval subsided in Devon, and Chagford sank back into agricultural peace. The following century and a half were years of gentle progress in the life of the parish. From the Restoration until 1800 the principal occupation of the parish was farming. The tin industry was no longer operative, for the surface deposits had been worked out and the remaining ore was extracted by shaft mining, which became the property of mining companies in the 18th century.

Spinning of wool for the woollen industry in north and east Devon remained a source of income for the parish until the early years of the 18th century when the Devon wool industry began to decline, and in the latter half of the century the prosperity of the Devon woollen towns became very much reduced. However, the industry stayed alive and may have created a certain amount of employment for Chagford spinners throughout the period.

Life on the farms changed slowly. Oxen, horses and men, in numbers we can no longer imagine, did the work of husbandry. A few new vegetables and fruits may have been added to the traditional crops. Westcote, writing in 1603, says of the Devon husbandmen:

> they have of late years much enlarged their orchards, and are very curious in planting and grafting all kinds of fruits, for all seasons, of which they make good use and profit, both for furnishing their own table as firnishing for the neighbour markets.
>
> But most especially for making of cider, a drink both pleasant and healthy; much desired of seamen for long southern voyages, as more fit to make beverage than beer, and much cheaper and easier to be had than wine.

In 1840 a third of the parish's farming land was arable, and if this was representative of the general trend in farming over the preceding century, we can imagine the amount of manual labour involved in ploughing, seeding and harvesting almost 3,000 acres of land. In addition, there was the haymaking, milking, and the perennial care of sheep, cattle, pigs and poultry. Hedges had to be cut and laid, walls repaired, gates mended, the garden and orchard tended, the bees to be taken care of. In the days before the Industrial Revolution all these jobs required separate skills and long hours of work for the farmer. According to Cromwell, Devon in the 17th century was the best farmed county in England, and perhaps this was the result of the tremendous effort needed to overcome the ruggedness and windswept quality of the land, but probably also a result of the large number of owner-occupied farms that had existed since medieval times in the county.

The Elizabethan age had created a rural prosperity that lasted through the 16th and 17th centuries and saw substantial rebuilding of the parish farmhouses. The Devon longhouse was still the traditional form for the farms of the parish. Many were improved or enlarged over the period. Hole was rebuilt in the 17th century, the date on the porch being 1668. Shapley was given the addition of an elaborate porch in 1776.

As befitted the character of the land, farming was mixed. Wheat, barley and oats, with relatively recent introduction of potatoes, probably absorbed the arable land. In the late 18th century the eastern edge of Dartmoor became famous for potato cultivation, largely because the farmers of south and west Devon were excluded by their leases from growing potatoes for sale. Potatoes from the Chagford region were taken by pack-horse to Two Bridges, where a market existed to provide for the needs of Plymouth and Tavistock.

Pack-horses were still used for transport of goods until the end of the 18th century. It was only in the early years of the 19th century that wagons came to be used on Dartmoor and its border parishes, which created the necessity of widening the lanes and the medieval bridges to allow through the wider form of transport.

For manuring his land the farmer had available dung, compost, ash and lime. Ash-houses, found near many of the parish's longhouses, not only provided for the storage of the ash in dry conditions, but also allowed for the removal of the hot ash left at the end of the day from the house itself, so reducing the risk of fire. A fine example stands beside the road at Nattadon. Lime was brought in by pack-horse; the Rev. John Swete describes in his journal for 1797 how he met a pack-horse train near Chagford which was bringing a supply of lime up from Ashburton.

Ploughing was done mainly by oxen, but some horses were now being used. Hoeing, reaping and binding was done by hand.

Probably most of the cattle were the ancestors of the South Devons, with some of the darker Devons or Ruby Reds bred in. These are the ideal native animals for the mixed farm, giving good quality milk and beef. The farms of the parish must have used these animals, probably with few exceptions, although in very varying quality, for pure breeds were only just beginning to be considered and a farmer would have done his best with the animals available.

Sheep were an important part of the farm economy in the days of the woollen trade, and again the flocks were probably the root stock of the present Dartmoor herds. Since they were grazed on the moorland slopes they had to be able to withstand the rough weather that the exposed hillsides are subject to.

Apart from the heavy working horses, Dartmoor ponies were used for transport, both ridden and pulling small carts and traps.

On the moorland, warrens of rabbits had been established in Norman times, for where these creatures could be contained they provided a valuable source of food.

Devonshire cream, cheese and butter, poultry, pigs, perhaps goats and bees all contributed to the rich life of the parish farms in those fertile days.

There were several corn mills in the parish. Holy Street mill, Yeo mill, Rushford mill, Sandy Park mill, and Batworthy mill all ground corn throughout this period and continued to do so in the 19th century.

Towards the end of the 18th century farming prosperity and the life of the farm labourer became harder. In many cases his wages were low and his food and keep inadequate.

Not only the farms, but the houses and cottages in the village were substantially built or rebuilt in this period. A considerable part of Chagford was burnt down at the end of the 17th century, and again in 1742 there was a fire in New Street. Granite, timber and thatch were all readily available for rebuilding, and new cottages and houses replaced those burnt down.

Fig. 5.   The Square, Chagford (from an etching by Samuel Prout)

The parish centred about the village, but consisted of many small hamlets that had grown out of medieval manors and the larger farms of the freeholders. Yet the farms and smallholdings of this period were often much smaller than they are today. Thus there are records of freeholders holding land at Middlecott, Stiniall, Yardworthy and other places, which means that they held land within the boundaries of that hamlet or manor. In the 18th century there were five farms listed at Yardworthy, four at Stiniall, and a variety of people held land at Westcott, Middlecote, Week and Easton.

Some of the old parish families had disappeared and new names had appeared to replace them. In 1664 John Prouz, the last male descendant of that family, died and the ancient line disappeared from the parish. A monument to the memory of John Prouz is in the south chancel of the church. Waye Barton became the property of the Courtenays, but was bought from them by John Collacott in the early years of the 18th century. John Collacott's daughter married one of the Northmores of Cleve. It was the Northmores who gained possession of Whyddon Park after the last of the Whyddons disappeared from the parish.

The Hayters were now in possession of the rectory, until in 1825 the last male descendant of the family died and the family became Hayter Hames.

The family of Rowe were at Holy Street until the early 19th century, when the heiress of that family married a Southmead, a family well established in the parish, and Holy Street became the property of John Rowe Southmead, their son.

Rushford was still the home of the Hore family until the death of Charles Hore in 1726 when that branch of the family died out.

The Ellis family had been in the parish since medieval times, originally having settled in the manor of Middlecott; in the early 19th century there were Ellises at Westcote, Great Week, and Stiniall.

The Nosworthies had also been established in the parish for some generations. The Clampitts became residents at Week.

The lordship of the manor went through several hands during this period. The lord of the manor no longer had the rights and duties of previous times, but he continued to be a protector of the village in certain respects, and Courts Leet and Courts Baron were held for Chagford until the end of the 19th century. The lord collected the 'High Rents' and at the court appointed a village constable (in the days before the creation of the police force). In 1820 at the Court Leet and Court Baron, John Ellis was appointed constable, James Rowe scavenger, William Scutt was appointed searcher and sealer of leather and William Short was breadweigher and aletaster. In this way law, order and regulation of quality in some important respects was catered for.

If the high rents were not paid the Steward of the Court might be authorised by the lord of the manor to hold cattle, goods and chattels until the arrears were made good.

After the Whyddon line came to an end, the lordship of the manor passed to one of the Courtenays. It was sold in 1706, after his death and divided into thirds, one third was sold to John Northcote of Chagford, butcher; one third to Oliver Woodley of Chagford of the same profession; and the last third to John Weekes of Chagford, yeoman. During the next century a series of marriages and sales found the manor in a variety of hands. In 1763 William Weekes, son of John, sold his share of the manor to John Coniam and by 1785 two thirds belonged to John Coniam and one third to John Southmead. Teigncombe had devolved into the manor of Collerew, and was held jointly with the manor of Chagford as though they were one.

Shapley manor was the property of the Prouz family until the 17th century, when it went to the Whyddons. In 1790 it was held by the Courtenays and then went through a series of sales so that in 1822 it was the property of Mr. Maunder of Exeter.

The manor of Rushford went from the Hores to the Northmores, and in 1822 was in the possession of John Hooper of South Teign.

The manor of South Teign, or the Prince's manor, was still in the possession of the Duchy of Cornwall. It had been held of the Duchy by the Whyddons in former times.

The Northmores owned a substantial amount of property in Chagford during the 19th century. They owned Whyddon House until they sold it to the Seymours. They owned Waye, which then passed to the Coniams. They had property at Westcote and at Colehole, and for a short time held the manors of Rushford and Shapley. But they were never really residents of the parish and by 1840 they had sold all their property.

Markets and fairs were held in the village. There was a Saturday market for meat, vegetables and farm produce and four cattle fairs during the year, which were held on the last Thursday in the months of March, September and October, and the first Thursday in May. The rights to these markets and fairs were still the property of the churchwardens for the parish. They must have provided a good outlet for surplus produce and a certain entertainment for the village.

The roads that served Chagford had altered very little, and it was only the introduction of horse carts and carriages some time around 1800 that brought a demand for wider roads and better surfaces. The lanes have changed their course very little since those times, but some have been enlarged and improved, so that their use has changed. In 1790 the usual route to Moretonhampstead was from the church down the hill to Westcott and Week and past Drewston, meeting the modern road at the parish boundary. The ancient trackway across the moor from Exeter was still the main road from Exeter to Chagford, passing through Dunsford and Drewsteingnton on its way.

Traffic, however, was increasing in the 18th century, and at last it became necessary to improve Devon's highways. The cost of laying tarmacadam on the highways was too great to be borne by the parishes and was financed by groups of landowners and businessmen, under Acts of Parliament, with capital loans, to be recouped by the use of turnpikes. It was through this system that the main highway across the moor became the road from Moretonhampstead to Tavistock, which was turnpiked in 1772, although the surface was probably not completed until near the end of the century.

The increased volume of traffic gave rise to new wayside inns to accommodate travellers. The *Warren House* inn, at that time called *Newhouse,* is shown on a map of 1765. Originally it stood on the other side of the road, but was burnt in a fire in 1845 and rebuilt on a slightly different site. With the creation of the shaft mines at Vitifer in the 19th century it gained an added trade from the tin workers there. Its name suggests that a rabbit warren was kept there, where it would be possible to contain the animals in the hard ground, through which it was difficult for them to burrow.

With the increase in highway traffic came the age of highway robbers. Tradition has it that Alfred Noyse's poem *The Highwayman* was written about Chagford. Anyone who remembers the lines 'the highwayman came riding, riding, riding, up to the old

Inn door', can imagine the clatter of hooves on the cobbles below the window of the *Three Crowns*, where Bess the landlord's daughter sat waiting. Certainly the lonely road from Beetor Cross to Tavistock would have provided good opportunities for the highwaymen.

There were several inns available to travellers to Chagford at that time. The Whyddon's house became the *Black Swan* and subsequently the *Three Crowns*; *Gregory's Arms* later became the *Globe*; the *King's Arms* is now *Lydstone*; the *Baker's Arms* is now the *Buller's Arms*; the *Royal Oak* is now the draper's shop, and the *Ring of Bells* is still extant. These inns and taverns seem to have come into being during the course of the 18th and early 19th centuries, as demand increased. They provided accommodation for travellers and their horses, and drinking places for the local population.

Drinking was common to both rich and poor. There were ample supplies of local beer and cider, and smuggling on the south coast doubtless brought in cheap wine, port, rum, or brandy. In these last days before Victorian Puritanism, when people still danced round the maypole on May morn, and tea drinking was considered a foreign and degenerate habit, there were doubtless many occasions when Chagford resounded with music, dancing, laughter, and tipsiness.

A slight decline in the prosperity of the farming industry was offset in Chagford by the opening of a woollen mill in 1800. Mr. Berry, finding labour scarce in Ashburton, moved to Chagford, and opened a mill near Chagford bridge. This enterprise manufactured blanket and serge, and at its height employed 1,200 weavers. Two buildings near the river, now Factory Cottages, with a building on the site of what is now *Moorlands* hotel, were the nucleus of the industry. The site near the river had originally been a corn mill, first mentioned in the 14th century. Although the conditions may have embodied some of the evils associated with the early days of the Industrial Revolution, poor conditions and long hours, it provided a necessary source of employment for many people.

Chagford was already on the main pack-horse route from Ashburton to North Devon, and transport of the finished cloth was aided by the introduction of waggons around the beginning of the 19th century. This in turn necessitated the widening of the parish bridges.

This new industry must have saved a large number of Chagford's population from poverty, that was at that time the terror of the working classes. The poor rates did something to help those who found themselves unable to provide for their families, but the poorhouse was the last resort and an alternative universally dreaded. The nearest poorhouse was then at Newton Abbot. It was a common arrangement that orphans and children of destitute families be apprenticed to some trade to save them from the workhouse or to bring them out of it when they reached a working age.

The charity known as Bunnamy's Bread originated in this period. From at least 1726, bread to the amount of £1 7s. 0d. was provided by the churchwardens of the parish every Good Friday out of the parochial funds in their hands, and was distributed by them in penny and twopenny loaves among poor persons of the parish, who attended for that purpose.

The new roads, with stage coaches, provided another new service: the delivery of mail. The Falmouth mail coach passed Crockernwell at about eight o'clock of the evening after it left London, and the letters it deposited there were taken to Moreton-hampstead. From there they were delivered to Chagford on Tuesdays and Saturdays. In 1842 a post office was opened in Chagford, after which letters arrived daily at 8 a.m. Letters mailed in London took 36 hours to reach Chagford, which must appear a very efficient service in the days before train, car or aeroplane. The letters were brought from Moretonhampstead by 'Foot Post' in the person of S. Gidley.

The woollen mill contributed to an increase in population in the early years of the 19th century. In 1801 it stood at 1,115; in 1821 the population had risen to 1,503. This increase in population and wealth gave rise to some new building. While many of the cottages may have been built at this time, it is certain that the 19th century saw the building of many new houses by the more prosperous members of the community. In 1820 Mr. Berry built a house in Mill Street, and it was at about this time that the Rev. William Hames built the new Chagford rectory, now Chagford House. In 1826 a fire at Waye Barton destroyed part of that house, giving rise to some rebuilding.

In 1831 the high rents of the manor of Chagford were paid for 35 houses in town, and this was not the full number, for some were in arrears.

Two new bridges were built in the early 19th century. In 1826 Cranaford bridge was constructed, and in 1829 Yeo bridge was built.

The church continued as the focus of the village, although few changes were made during the period. In 1706 and 1766 six new bells were hung, and in 1762 a new font of Portland stone was erected at the cost to the parish of £3 3s. 0d. This replaced the ancient granite font to be discovered a century later.

The manorial chapels had by now disappeared. The chapel of St. Julian at Teign-combe was gone, along with the chapel of St. Mary at Week. The latter must have been finally demolished during the 17th century, for tradition had it that it was the Whyddons misfortune to have used the stones, and they disappeared from the parish soon after the Restoration.

Major Hore was responsible for removing the chapel at Rushford, because 'it obscured his view'. The stones were rebuilt into the orchard wall, where a few can be discerned today. In defence of Major Hore it should be said that Westcote, in 1630, said that the chapel at Rushford was 'long since decayed, in whose ruins grew an oak which always bore white leaves'.

It was the early years of the 19th century that saw the removal of the crosses from the village square by the lords of the manor. Again this may have been partially the result of wider and more unmanoeuverable traffic. An ancient oak cross tree on the north side of the square was also removed at this time.

Chagford had its share of craftsmen and tradesmen. There were wheelwrights and a cooper. There were butchers, blacksmiths and bakers, a substantial number of boot and shoe makers, and of carpenters. There were grocers, drapers, tailors and saddlers. Each of the mills had a miller and there were, of course, large numbers of weavers and spinners at the mill.

By the beginning of Victoria's reign there was also a watch and clock maker; there were ironmongers, and a brazier.

In 1790 John Weekes left £200 in four per cent. stock to be applied for the schooling and apprenticeship of poor children. This was the first provision for schooling made in the parish.

The weather must at times have been harsh. In 1827 the Teign was frozen over at Chagford bridge, and this may not be the only time that it happened. Without doubt the same discontent, worry and grumbles about the state of the weather were heard throughout the parish.

International and even national events caused little disturbance. A Church of England and Protestant succession had been assured for the monarchy, and the gentle low church land of the Hayter and Hames family kept the church in Chagford on an even course.

The loss of the American colonies in 1776 may have had an effect on trade, and the war with France saw the building of the prison at Princetown, with a railway soon to follow; but even Princetown was a good journey from Chagford at the beginning of the 19th century.

The 18th century must have been a peaceful time for rural Devon. The squire, the rector, and the country gentry gave an air of peaceful solidarity that seemed unchangeable. The farmers were prosperous and provided a wide variety of foods for the local markets. The spate of building gave better housing, and to the craftsmen a good trade. As always it was the labouring population who suffered the worst or the setbacks and whose fortunes rested so delicately on the state of the local economy. When times were hard, it was they who went hungry, and had it not been for poor relief and a certain reasonable generosity of those more fortunate than themselves, their lives would often have been harder.

Yet in a population as small and as isolated as Chagford there was probably a certain amount of caring by the parish for its own. As a smaller unit than the parish, the families of the gentry gave a clannish protection to their servants and labourers, many of whom stayed with them all their lives.

For social equality or for adventure the 18th century in Chagford has little to offer, but it gives a feeling of fertility, peace and stability that have long since disappeared.

Chapter Twelve

CHAGFORD FAMILIES

THE NAME CHAGFORD denotes a place, but its life is the life of its people. The connection between land and people was so strong and so enduring in medieval times that families were usually known by the name of the manor or freehold that they inhabited. Hence we read of the family of de Chagford, who owned that manor in the early medieval period, the de Risfords at Rushford, William de Yeo, Robert atte Thorn and the family of Teigncombe. The Endacotts were originally at Yondecott in South Tawton.

Many of the family names well-known in Chagford today date back to medieval times. Devon is notoriously slow to change, and its people reluctant to move. Although the rapid communications of the 20th century have seen a greater immigration from the county, many of Chagford's inhabitants have remained rooted in the ancient parish. In moving, Devonians have seldom moved far, often to a neighbouring parish or to another part of the county.

Some of Chagford's families have gone into the female line once, perhaps many times, but the connections with the parish remain unbroken. A few families, once well-known, have disappeared from the area only to surface again in the United States, Canada, or Australia. With a touching patriotism for their roots, members of these families return to visit the parish to re-establish their connections.

Of the families whose names are also those of farms and manors, none now remain on their original holdings. The de Chagfords went into the female line in the 14th century. The de Risford's heiress married into the family of Hore, and the manor passed into that line in the time of Richard II.

The Monke family were at Rushford in the 14th and 15th centuries, and must have held the manor from the Hores. By Tudor times the Hores were themselves resident.

The Courtenays held land in the parish at various times in their long history. In 1428 Johanna Countenay held the manor of Shapley, and in 1446 one of the Courtenays was granted the manor of Teigncombe for life. By 1554 Peter Courtenay held Broadweke, Middlecott, and Yardworthy. In the 17th century Philippa Prouz, the daughter of John Prouz, the last male of that line, married Richard Courtenay, and Waye Barton was, for a short time, the property of that gentleman. The manor of Chagford passed into their hands in the late 17th century, but was soon sold.

In 1378 there was already a family of Elys within the manor of Middlecott, and this family has retained its connections to the present day. In the 17th century there were Ellises at Yellam and Middlecott, and in the 18th century the same family owned Thorn and part of Stiniall. In 1903 Mrs. Mary Elizabeth Ellis inherited Waye Barton, along with the manors of Chagford and Collerewe from her father, Thomas Taylor Coniam.

There were Wekes in the parish in the 15th century, and they must have originally belonged at Weeke, although of this I can find no record. The family of Thorn, in similar fashion, are descended from Robert atte Thorn, who farmed at Thorn in the 14th century and whose family in all probability originally created the foundations of that hamlet.

From the 14th century there are records of the family of Aysshe in Chagford, Tonker at Frenchbear, Cole at Southulle (Southill), Richard Northull and Alexander Stoneman at Northull (Northill), John Newcombe at Yeo, and Hugh Tappelagh within the manor of Teigncombe. By 1434 there was a Pyreman (Perryman), at Frenchbear, and this family acquired Yeo in the following century, and Southill in the 17th century.

The medieval years were dominated by the family of Prouz of Gidleigh, and those other great medieval families of Bonville, Wibbery and Gorges, to which they were related. The family of Prouz appeared in Gidleigh soon after the Norman Conquest, establishing themselves at Gidleigh Castle. It was in 1345 that Robert de Waye released all his right of land in Chagford to William Prouz, a younger son of the Gidleigh knights.

The Gidleigh branch of the family went into the female line in the 14th century and the manor and Castle of Gidleigh became the possession of the de Moelys family through the marriage of Alice Prouz to Roger de Moelys. The Chagford branch of the family, however, flourished and remained the oldest and most stable of Chagford's nobility until the 17th century. The churchwarden's accounts are full of the names of the many members of the family who held office as churchwardens, contributed to the many community projects and were baptized, wed and finally buried in Chagford church.

Yet it was through the Gidleigh branch of the family, in particular Isolda, the daughter of Alice Prouz and Roger de Moelys, that the manor of Chagford passed to the Wibberys. Isolda married Oliver (de Wibbery) of Chagford, the heir of Thomas de Chagford and John de Wibbery, and, passing through this line, the manor went to the great heiress, Leva Gorges, to her daughter, Joan, who married a Bonville, and so to Joan's daughter, Anna, who married Philip Coplestone. In seven generations the manor of Chagford passed through the hands of five of Devon's greatest medieval families. By the time that the Tudor age dawned all these families had been swallowed by the upheaveals of the Wars of the Roses and the beginning of a new age for England. The Bonvilles had descended to Cecily, the last of her line, described as the greatest heiress of her day, who married Thomas Grey, 1st Marquis of Dorset, and one of the new nobility.

The Coplestones retained Chagford until the rise of a new family absorbed the manor and advowson of Chagford. The Whyddons were the strongest family of the Tudor age in Chagford; in a sense they typified the change in social structure that occurred at that time and, surviving the age of the Stuarts, they then declined and disappeared.

Due to the increase of documentation, in particular the beginning of the church-warden's accounts, from 1480 onwards a world of familiar and now less familiar names open up. Apart from the Prouz family at Waye, the Whyddons at Easton, and the Hores at Rushford, we can at least list the names of many families and in some cases place them in their respective homes.

The Endacotts appear at Drewston, with some land in Middlecott. The Yoldens were within the manor of Middlecott and later at Week.

The Knapmans, a family who probably made their fortune in tin, owned Broad-withecombe and Withecombe, acquired Yardworthy from the Countenays, and also possessed Rushford Wood.

In 1545 the Perrymans moved to Yeo and it may well be this family who built the mill there, originally used for threshing and grinding corn. They moved to Yeo from Frenchbear, which later became the property of the Hores, and in 1655 Southill was also the Perryman's.

The Battishall family were widespread in the parishes of South Tawton, Drewsteign-ton and Spreyton before this time, but in 1563 one of the family claimed Colehall from the Verwylls and have been in the parish ever since.

The Taverners owned Yellam and sold it to Robert Foxford in 1566, who sold it, two days later, to Sir John Whyddon, making himself the handsome profit of £5. He bought Yellam for £27 and sold it for £32.

Sir John Shilston of Shilston in Drewsteignton held Middlecott, part of Yardworthy and Great Week during his life. He died in 1530.

John Seynthill held land in Ford and Ayreston (Easton) in the manor of South Teign, and sold them in 1539 to John Newcombe.

Robert Cornishe held Drewston and Hampton Weke in the 16th century and it was probably he who sold Drewston to the Endacotts.

The Northcotts claimed rights to Padley and Nattadon Commons from Henry Week in 1558 and this family had probably been in the parish some time. John Northcott leased Bellacouch in the 17th century from the Coplestones.

Yardworthy was a hamlet, rather than a farm at this time, hence various references to its ownership, for several families held land there. The Aysshe family, who are first recorded in Chagford in the 14th century, sold their share of Yardworthy to William Nosworthie in 1616. In the same year William Nosworthie had acquired Hole from John Laskey, and half of Corendon from William Aysshe.

The Rowes were probably already at Holy Street, where they remained until the 18th century.

The Yolland family were at Week and were probably a tin-mining family. They remained in the parish until the 18th century.

Tne rents of the church house and St. Katharine's house, along with the field of St. Katharine's Hay, provide several more names.

The church house was leased in the 15th century to William Yolland, and in the 16th century to John Verycomb, Richard Clyffe, and then to the Whyddons. St. Katharine's house was leased to Nicholas Podycomb and later to Gabriel Agatt. St. Katharine's Hay was rented out to John Grose and then to William Body.

Of the other family names from the Tudor period, I can find no records to place them. Many of these names appear today and some seem to reappear in altered forms. We hear of Bennet, Hodge, Favell or Fanell, Tappelegh, Vallance, Hooper, Wills,

Denford, Hext, Clampitt and Rugg. There are Jorstons, probably still at Jurston, there are French, Potter, Dunning, Walcote and Westcote, Hill, Splott, Rise (presumably now Rice), Neck and Dodd. Smyth, Trend, Gearde, Byrd and Northway were all present.

In 1607 a survey was made of the manor of South Teign and at this time the following people held the following property:

The principal landowner was Sir John Whyddon (not the judge, but his grandson), who held 800 acres. Thorn in Easton was divided between Thomas Collihall, Stephen Bennet, and Oliver and Francis Whyddon, with a cottage and meadow called Broad Mead held by Elizabeth Knapman and Margaret Newcombe (daughters of William Newcombe).

Thomas Bennet held Shutt in Easton, which was 30 acres, and John Nosworthie held a tenement in Easton. Nicholas Laskie held a close of land named Whiteaberry. Philip Smyth held a tenement in Westcott. Thomas Bennet, John Wills, Thomas Yolden, John Hooper and Edward Denford held tenements in Week. Edward Ellis had a tenement in Ellam and some land in Middlecott. Edward Furlong and Robert Claffe held Meacombe, Thomas Crowte held Horselake, Robert Foxford held Thorne in Easton, John Endacott held Drewston, although Thomas Taverner held part of Drewston's land and John Cornishe owned a piece of land called Slankcombe.

All these tenants of the Crown were free tenants. Since it was still a royal manor, the tenants were free from toll and ferry charges, free from contributions to repairing bridges and walls, and from payment for grazing cattle in the royal forest. They were also free of toll in all markets and fairs throughout England. In addition they were at liberty to fish the river within the manor as they would.

The 18th century saw little movement of peoples and few new families seem to have appeared in the parish at that time. The Northmore family acquired a considerable amount of property from the decline of the Whyddons, but they were based at Cleve, outside Exeter and never really became residents of the parish.

The Clampitt family increased their holding and acquired part of the manors of Chagford and Collerewe in the 19th century. It was during the 18th century that the Coniams seem to have appeared, and they became part owners of the lordship of the manor in 1763. By the end of the following century the manor was entirely theirs and passed through the marriage of Thomas Taylor Coniam's eldest daughter to the name of Ellis. The Ellis family had belonged in Chagford since at least the 14th century and it seems right that the manor should finally come to such an ancient name.

The Southmead family came from Wraye Barton in Moretonhampstead, but John Southmead married Lydia Rowe and Holy Street became the home of the Rowe-Southmeads.

The Collacott family owned Waye Barton in the middle of the 18th century, from them it went to the Coniams.

In 1775 William Yeo of Plymouth sold Hampton Weeke to William Ellis, and the Ellises retained this connection with Week until the present time. William Yeo may have been descended from the medieval family of Yeo, situated at the place of that name, that later became the home of the Perrymans.

From the 17th century a few other names are added. Tapper, Denham, Seaward and Bowden are present. The Devon Protestation Returns of 1642 give a fairly complete list of the names of the menfolk of the parish and the list is reproduced at the end of this chapter.

The 17th century also saw the advent of the Hayters at the parsonage, every generation of this family providing at least one rector of the parish, until they merged into Hames. The tradition of a Hayter Hames rector ended in Victorian times, but the family remains.

The tithe map apportionment gives a list, with properties, of the landowners of the parish, which is also reproduced here.

The 19th century saw the beginning of the great migrations that have only accelerated in the 20th century. It would be futile to try and list these endless comings and goings, for they represent no continuity, but only the restless tides of modern fortunes. Many of the people who came and settled, often only to leave again, made wonderful contributions to the life of the parish and have appeared in their respective chapters. But they are not yet the living blood of the parish. To justify my remark, I can quote from a newspaper article at the wedding of my grandparents, which described my grandfather as belonging to an old family from Wiltshire. At the time the family had been in Chagford for nearly 300 years and the parishioners had, in their presentation to the bridegroom, spoken of him as being 'a most worthy representative of an old and much respected family long resident among us'. In 1897, 300 years of 'residence among us' does not quite seem to be 'of the parish'. However much we might resent this attitude, it gives full tribute to the rooting of man on his soil, which is the finest feature of rural Devon life.

Although it is not always possible to place families on their farms, in their cottages or even to their occupations, their names are there. Their work is seen in the houses, cottages, walls and hedges of the parish, and though I cannot name the builders, where it is possible I will try to give some indication of the history of the parish's buildings.

Of those farms and houses built in the medieval period, none can remain in their original condition. The longhouse was built to accommodate men, women, children and cattle, but the cattle have been relegated to their own accommodation, while that of the people has been altered and improved. Yardworthy farm still contains a porch and wall of an early medieval longhouse, though this is no longer incorporated into the present farmhouse.

Holy Street was first built in the 11th century, but the oldest part of the present house is probably Tudor and extremely beautiful.

Hurston and Jurston, Yeo and Thorn were all farms with houses in the medieval period. Of these, Thorn was rebuilt in the 17th century, as in all probability were the others. Hole was an ancient farmstead, rebuilt in 1668. Collihole, equally an old settlement, has been rebuilt, possibly later.

East and West Combe, Corndon, Drewston, Easton, Forder, Frenchbear, Middlecott, Northill, Shapley, Stiniall, Southill, Teigncombe, Week, Withecombe and Yellam were all farms with houses in the medival period. They were probably all substantially rebuilt or re-converted in the 18th century. Shapley has an 18th-century porch, Lower Withecombe an ornate plaster ceiling. Frenchbear was finally rebuilt in the early years of the 20th century by Robert Stark.

Waye Barton was equally medieval, but its oldest existing wing is Tudor and doubtless built by the Prouz family.

Rushford Barton was a 16th-century Barton, or larger farmhouse, until it was burnt down in 1913 and was almost completely rebuilt.

Whyddon House was built in 1649, but the interior has been rearranged by countless inhabitants, although the oak panelling and spiral staircase remain original and very fine.

Batsworthy mill and Rushford mill were both in existence in the 15th century, but both have been considerably altered since. Sandy Park mill only ceased to grind corn in the 20th century, and is now the *Mill End* hotel. It has been changed a great deal, but some of the interior woodwork is old enough to be original.

Although Nattadon Common is mentioned in early records, the farm is not. It may well be a 16th- or 17th-century encroachment on the moorland, and the house probably dates from this time.

Within the village, the church remains supreme. The interior changes have not altered the original exterior, which displays, like so many of Devon's churches, its Norman origins.

The Bishop's House is almost certainly late medieval; some of the cottages in New Street are 15th-century, and a few may be older. The *Three Crowns* and the similar thatched buildings adjoining it are early Tudor. Bellacouch dates from the same time and was probably built by the Coplestones.

Orchard Cottage must be the site of the original Chagford Manor Farm, but its building does not display this antiquity.

The majority of the cottages in the parish have been brought up-to-date in recent times. Yet they still retain their granite walls, oak beams and, in some cases, thatched roofs. Building styles altered so little between the 16th and the 19th centuries that, while it is possible to place them within that period, it would take a greater specialist than I to date them more exactly. Within the town, many of the dwellings retain their courtyards, hidden behind the cottages themselves, which were the cottagers' version of a farmyard in those days.

The Victorian age saw a radical change in building styles and a great increase in house building. Slate roofs appeared, courtyards disappeared and the age of the town house dawned. The 'market house' in the centre of the Square, many of the houses in Mill Street, and Moor Park and Moorlands were built.

The spate of building, then begun, has continued through the 20th century, and shows itself in the character of the houses now displayed.

It is not possible to record all the names of Chagford's early inhabitants. Where they have not been involved in litigation or where their holdings are unrecorded, it is difficult to trace them. The buildings that they constructed and in which they lived will have to speak for them.

PROTESTATION RETURNS FOR CHAGFORD, 1642

Adams, Edward	Caseley, Barnabas	Harris, George
Aggett, Edward	Caseley, John	Harris, John
Aggett, John	Caseley, Peter	Harris, John
Aggett, Richard	Caseley, William	Harris, Walter
Aggett, Thomas	Caseley, William	Harston, Robert
Aggett, William	Cater, George	Hartt, John
Aish, William	Cater, George	Hill, David
Allen, John	Cater, Gregory	Hill, Nicholas
Aller, William	Chinge, Roger	Hodge, William
Anthony, Richard	Clampitt, Hugh	Hole, Francis
Arscott, John	Clement, John	Hole, John
Arscott, Robert	Cliffe, John	Hole, William
Aynell, James	Cliffe, William	Hooper, Henry
Baron, Edward	Collihole, George	Hooper, Henry
Baron, George	Cooper, Walter	Hooper, Richard
Baron, George	Copplestone, John, gent.	Hooper, Thomas
Baron, John	Corne, John	Hooper, William
Bennett, Edward	Crediford, John	Horsman, Nicholas
Bennett, James	Croote, Thomas	Horwill, Hannibal
Bermett, Richard	Cullicott, Oliver	Hunt, Edward
Berry, Henry	Cullicott, Thomas	Hunt, Richard
Binny, John	Curry, William	James, Oliver
Bishopp, Edward	Dart, John	Joslyn, Richard
Bishopp, Thomas	Demon, Richard	Kenser, Bennett
Bishopp, William	Denceham, Richard	Kinge, William
Blackaller, George	Denham, Gilbert	Knapman, Richard
Blight, John	Denham, John, gent.	Knowle, Richard
Body, Evens	Dicker, Edward	Knowle, Thomas
Body, John	Dininge, John	Lake, Alexander
Body, John	Dodd, Anthony	Lake, William
Body, Walter	Dodd, Richard	Langford, William, gent.
Body, William	Dodde, Gregory	Langworthy, Henry
Body, William	Dodde, John	Langworthy, John
Bonamy, Edward	Duninge, Richard	Langworthy, William
Bonamy, John	Elles, Robert	Lashbrook, Edward
Bowden, Nicholas	Ellis, James	Leeve, John
Box, Richard	Ellis, John	Leman, William
Bremelcombe, John	Ellis, Nicholas	Lightfoote, John
Bremelcombe, William	Ellis, William	Lopas, Gilbert
Brocke, George	Endicott, Henry	Lopas, Robert
Brocke, John	Endicott, Henry	Lopas, William
Brocke, Oliver	Endicott, Richard	Losber, Laurence
Brocke, Thomas	Endicott, Robert	Loskey, Alexander
Burridge, Roger	Fowell, John	Loskey, Peter
Butcher, Alexander	Germyn, William	Loskey, William
Butcher, Richard	Gervis, William	Luce, Henry
Can, Oliver	Grosse, John	Lyne, John
Can, William	Grosse, Nicholas	Maine, Baldwyn
Canne, Thomas	Grosse, Oliver	March, Thomas
Carry, James	Grosse, William	Marck, George
Carry, John	Hanson, John	Martyn, Robert
Caseley, Barnard	Hanworthy, Henry	Martyn, Robert
Caseley, John	Hanworthy, Richard	Masy, John

Protestation Returns for Chagford, 1642—*continued*

Maunder, Richard
May, Gregory
May, Roger
May, William
More, Laurence
Mylles, John
Necke, Thomas
Northcote, Robert
Northcott, John
Noseworthy, John
Noseworthy, Richard
Noseworthy, William
Nosworthy, John
Nosworthy, Thomas
Orchard, John
Paddicombe, Stephen
Paule, William
Paule, William
Perryman, Mathias
Peryman, Thomas
Peryman, William
Peryman, William
Petheridge, Hugh
Pethebridge, William
Petter, John
Pole, Gilbert
Potter, James
Prach, John, gent.
Prach, Nicholas, gent.
Puddicombe, John
Puddicombe, Nicholas
Rennolls, William
Ribley, Richard
Ripley, Richard
Rooke, Philip
Rowe, John
Rugge, Arthur
Salter, Nicholas
Sarell, John
Saunder, Alexander
Scatte, Gregory
Scatte, Gilbert

Scatte, William
Scutte, Gilbert
Searle, John
Seyward, John
Seyward, Roger
Shapter, Henry
Simons, John
Sleepe, John
Smith, John
Smith, William
Soper, Gregory
Soper, Gregory
Soper, John
Soper, William
Spears, John
Splatt, John
Splatte, Bennett
Stotte, John
Stronge, William
Stronge, William
Syres, John
Tancombe, John
Tapper, Thomas
Taverner, Peter
Taverner, William
Taylor, John
Toser, John
Toser, John
Trend, Diggory
Trend, Gregory
Trend, John
Trend, Richard
Trend, William
Trend, William
Tuckett, Christopher
Turner, Roger
Uppacott, Robert
Vallance, Peter
Vallance, William
Varder, John
Varder, Laurence
Varder, Oliver

Varder, Richard
Varder, Thomas
Venicomb, Glyn
Vougewill, John
Vougewill, John
Vougewill, Henry
Vougewill, John
Vougewill, John
Vougewill, John
Vougewill, Thomas
Vougewill, William
Wannell, Anthony
Wannell, Oliver
Wannell, Richard
Wannell, Richard
Weekes, Barnabas
Weekes, James
Weekes, Richard
Weekes, William
Weekes, William
Weekes, William
Westeway, Robert
Whealer, James
Whiddon, John, gent.
Whiddon, John, gent.
Whiddon, Rowland, Esq.
Whiddon, William
Whiteway, John
Willes, Henry
Willes, Henry
Willes, Thomas
Willes, Thomas
Williams, Valentine
Wolcott, William
Woodleigh, John
Woodley, Edward
Woodley, Oliver
Woodly, William
Yolden, Stephen
Toldon, Thomas
Youlden, John

Signatures:

John Denham, Clerk
Alexander Trend, Constable
John Walter, Constable
Thomas Dodd, Churchwarden
Gilbert Northcott, Churchwarden
John Dodd, Overseer
John Trend, Overseer

1439
November 12.
Westminster.

To the escheator in Devon. Order to take the fealty of Joan daughter of John Wibbury, and to give her seisin of the moieties of the manor and advowson of Aveton Gyffards and of the advowson of the chantry of Lyneton at the altar of St. Mary in that church, but to remove the king's hand and meddle no further with a moiety of the manor of Stodbury and with a water mill in Chaggeforde, delivering to her any issues thereof taken; as it is found by inquisition, taken before John Coplestone late escheator, that Richard Hankeforde and Henry Foleforde then deceased and Nicholas Tremayne then living were seised of the moieties aforesaid, and by charter indented, dated Aveton Gyffarde 22 November 4 Henry V, demised the same to John Wibbury for life, by name of John Wibbury esquire, with remainder to Lena his wife while sole, to find all children of her begotten by him, with the issues, revenues and profits thereof and of the manor of Chaggeforde and all messuages, lands, rents, services and reversions of all tenants in Chaggeforde and Colerewe, all lands etc in Stotescombe and Holbogheton and a close in Holbogheton called 'Smytheswillesparke', all late of John Wibbury, so that if she should take another husband all should remain to the heirs of the said John's body with the remainder for lack of such issue to the said Lena for life, under condition that she should yearly find a chaplain to celebrate in this parish church of 'Liteltoriton' for his soul and the souls of his parents, ancestors, friends and benefactors, entailing the fee simple as he or his heirs by writings or testatment should declare, that by virtue of that demise John Wibbury was seised of the premises as of freehold, and died so seised, that the said Lena was great with child by him, and was then sole and unmarried, neither was she ever married after his death, that John Wibbury died seised of the said mill in his demesne as of fee, that the moieties of the manor of Aveton Gyffarde and of the said advowsons are held by knight service of Thomas son and heir of Hugh Courtenay earl of Devon, lately a minor in ward of the king, as of his castle of Plympton, and the moiety of the manor of Stodbury and the said mill of others than the king or the said heir, that the said Lena was great with child by him, and that such child if born would be his next heir; and by another inquisition, taken before Thomas Wyse esquire late escheator, it is likewise found that the daughter borne him by the said Lena, named Joan, was of full age on the feast of St. Lawrence last, and that on Sunday after the Invention of Holy Cross 3 Henry VI the said Lena took to her husband Thomas Bonvyle esquire yet living; and the said Joan proved her age before Thomas Wyse.

1840 TITHE COMMUTATION

	Owner	Occupier
Whiddon Park	Edward Baily Seymour	George Webber
Coombe	John Berry	John Berry
Town Mill Estates	John Berry	John Berry
Batworthy	John Broch	John Ellis
Stinial	John Broch	John Ellis
Lower Jurston	John Broch	John Ellis
Higher Drewston	Richard Broch	
Hole & Collihole	John Battishall	Henry Scott
Teigncombe	John Bennet	Alexander Holmes
Collyhole	John Cole	Robert Hellyer
Thornworthy	John Courtier	John Courtier
Great Frenchbeer	Frances Mary Clapp	John Stanbury
Higher Withecombe	Mary Cole	Richard Born
Waye Barton	John Coniam	John Coniam
Bellacouch	Suzanna Coniam	Suzanna Coniam
Westcott	Suzanna Coniam	Peter Farr
Combe	Nicholas Clampitt	Richard Wreyford

1840—Tithe Commutation—*continued*

	Owner	Occupier
Singmoor	Nicholas Clampitt	James Collins
Quintatown	William Clampitt	James Collins
Yellands	William Clampitt	James Collins
Lower Middlecott	William Clampitt	James Collins
Sparkes Middlecott	James Carter	James Rowe
Lower Horselake	James Carter	James Rowe
Catherine Hay	Churchwardens	William Ellis
Hurston	John Dodd	John Northcott
Town Tenement (part)	William Dicks	Samuel Hunt
Town Tenement (part)	William Dicks	Henry Hooper
Town Tenement (part)	William Dicks	John Broch
Middle Drewston	Catherine Dicker	Catherine Dicker
Lower Waddicott	Catherine Dicker	George Wills
Quintatown	Catherine Dicker	George Wills
Middle Middlecott	Trustees of Earl of Devon	Gabriel Clampitt
Buda	Catherine O'Brien	James Dodd
Higher Easton and Whiteaberry	Catherine O'Brein	James Nixon Cross
Quintatown	Rev. William Ponsford	John Hooper
Higher Withecombe	George Ponsford	William Ellis
Yeo	John Perryman	John Perryman
Wolfall & Wolford	John Perryman	John Perryman
Corndon	George Perryman	George Perryman
Collyhole	James Rowe	James Rowe
Forder	John Rowe	Richard Harvey, Jnr.
Perryman's Easton	Andrew Rowe	John Rowe
Part of Great Easton	John Rowe	John Rowe
Marches & Weeks Tenement	John Rowe	John Rowe
Great Easton	George Rowe	George Rowe
Jacob Parks	George Rowe	George Rowe
Holy Street	John Courtier & Jacharias Rendall	Clampitt
	(devisees of late Judith Southmead)	Richard Wreyford
Holy Street Mill	as above	Edward Aggett
Thorne	Thomas Stanbury	George Endacott
Little Stinial	John Scott (Scutt)	William Floud
Middle Corndon	John Scutt	John Scutt
Higher Shapley	Henry Soper	Henry Soper
Higher Weddicott	William Strong	William Strong
Broadlands	William Strong	John Brock
Lower & Middle Batworthy	Richard Savery	William Collins
Laskeys Ground	Peter Tarr	Peter Tarr
Cross' Tenement	Dinah Taylor	John Barnes
Penn	James Windeat	Alexander Holmes
Lower Hurston & Ridge Ley	John Wills	Joseph Northway
Higher Middlecott	John Yolland	James Rowe
Little Shapley	John Yolland	James Dodd
Glebe	Rev. William Hames	Rev. William Hames
Great Week	William Ellis	William Ellis
Little Week	John Ellis	John Ellis
Adley Meadows	John Ellis	John Crispin
Lower Drewston	Anthony Ellis	Anthony Ellis

1840—Tithe Commutation—*continued*

	Owner	Occupier
Stinial	William Ellis	William Ellis
Wolfeshall	Peter Ellis, Jnr.	Peter Ellis, Jnr.
Southill	Peter Ellis, Jnr.	Peter Ellis, Jnr.
Rushford Mill	Newton Fellowes	Peter Farr
Rushford Barton	Newton Fellowes	William Hooper
Corndon	Humphrey Harvey	Humphrey Harvey
Little Frenchbeer	Richard Harvey	George Mortimer
Fellowes Easton	Richard Harvey	Richard Harvey
Lakeland	John Hooper	Richard Harvey
Higher Jurston	John Hooper	John Harvey
Yellam & Wood Town	Henry and Ann Hooper	Henry Hooper
Greater Stone	Lydia Hooper	Lydia Hooper
Seawards Week	Lydia Hooper	Lydia Hooper
Great Week	Lydia Hooper	Lydia Hooper
Stinial	Lydia Hooper	Charlotte Boyer
Withecombe	John Hooper, Jnr.	John Hooper, Jnr.
Washfords	John Hooper, Suzanna Brock and Maria Northway	James Morrish
Cleaves	Mary Anne Hooper and Suzanna Temple	Richard Harvey
Wood Town	William Heywood	William Heywood
Higher Horselake	Suzanna Harvey	Susanna Harvey
Westcott Parks	Rev. William Hames	Rev. William Hames
Tunnafords	John Mare	George Herywarde
Broadlands and Piecend	William Nosworthy	William Nosworthy
Sandy Park Mill	Joseph Nichles	William Snow
Down Park	John Northway	William Floud
Whiddons Teigncombe	William Northcott	William Northcott
Teigncombe	William Northcott	Thomas Northcott
North Hill	William Northcott	William Northmore
Little Thorne	William Northcott	Richard Luscombe
Yardworthy	Simon Newcombe Neck	William Bowdin
Yardworthy	Simon Newcombe Neck	Simon Newcombe Neck
Metherall	Simon Newcombe Neck	Richard Wreyford and Clampitt

Chapter Thirteen

THE VICTORIAN ERA

WHEN THE YOUNG VICTORIA came to the throne of England in 1837 a revolution was beginning. It was a revolution full of contradictions between radical ideas in science, technology and natural history, and stringent rules of social conduct, moral values and religious ideals. Chagford saw its full share of the changes that the 19th century underwent, lived out those many contradictions and perhaps for the first time was penetrated by the life of the faster world outside. By the end of the century Chagford had ceased to be an isolated village on the edge of a wilderness and had become a neat little town visited by gentry and artists from many parts of England. Communications had broken through and times necessarily changed.

The Tithe Commutation Act might not seem like a radical event in England's history, yet it altered one of the basics of English rural life. Ever since the foundation of the Christian Church, the congregation had contributed to the upkeep of the rector by gifts in kind of their yearly produce. In this way the rector was tied into the agricultural life of his parish as surely as were the farmers and cottagers. By the time that the tithes were commuted for money sums it is probably true that many gifts were not made in kind, yet the Act finally stopped them. In addition, in order to make the new system completely clear, the tithe commissioners had drawn up complete and detailed maps of every parish in the country, accompanied by lists of every owner and occupier with a record of their buildings and acreages. The tithe map of Chagford was drawn up in 1840 and gives an excellent reference for the layout and ownership of the parish land and houses. How the Domesday clerks would have envied those perfect maps and neat lists in copperplate handwriting.

The total titheable acreage of the parish was 6,714 acres. Of this 2,965 was arable land, 776 was meadow and pasture, 64 was orchard, 173 acres was woodland, 889 was furzeland, and 1,997 was common land. A third was arable land and this was compensated for, despite the very small acreage of meadow and pasture, by the furzeland and common land which could not be claimed back from the moor and which supported much of the parish's livestock.

By the end of the century farming patterns had considerably altered and much of the arable land had been laid down to grass. The end of the Napoleonic Wars began a recession in agriculture, which never really picked up during the remainder of the century. The life of the farm labourer was hard in those times and helped to encourage a drift towards the towns, where growing industry and commerce promised a richer life. In 1840 the chief grain crop was wheat and this continued to be the case until the great agricultural depression of the 1870s and 1880s. At this time the arable land

103

returned to grass and wheat acreages fell below those of oats. Cattle and sheep took the place of grain, and this was the period when herds of South Devon cattle and of Ruby Reds became true breeds in the modern sense. Even after the closing of the woollen mill in the middle of the century and the collapse of that industry in Devon, sheep continued to be an important part of the farms' economy, for sheep naturally prefer well-drained slopes and rocky moorland.

The farms stretched perhaps a little further into the moorland; some land that was taken into cultivation during the century fell back into open moorland in the depression of the 1880s. The valley of the South Teign, now obscured by Fernworthy and blocked from the higher moor, was at that time still partially farmland. The lane to Metherall continued to the farm at Fernworthy, crossed the river and continued to Teign Head Farm, where a clump of trees protected this isolated holding from some of the south-westerly gales.

The 19th century saw the introduction of new machinery on the farms. Improved harrows, with cast-iron rollers, and later threshing-machines appeared, and at the end of the century mowing-machines were introduced. Iron production, and then the invention of new methods of producing steel meant an improvement and greater availability of farm implements and tools. Waggons and carts were now a feature of Chagford life and made the importing of such commodities as lime and the exporting of produce faster and more convenient.

Farming methods were not revolutionised—they were speeded up. The Chagford farmer's wife still tended calves and poultry, and still scalded milk at the kitchen fire to make her Devonshire cream.

In some of the larger houses the kitchen range had replaced the open fire as a means of cooking, but despite the greater control of heat it gave the cook, it required hard hours of scrubbing to keep it clean and shining.

The principal landowners in the parish at this time were the rectors and lords of the manor. In 1847 the rector was the Rev. William Hames, who had been rector of the parish for 17 years, and who was to hold the living until 1852, when he resigned in favour of his son, Hayter George. Between them, father and son occupied the living for 66 years, providing a continuity of paternal guidance to the parish, christening their children, marrying the young people, and burying the dead.

The tithes of the parish brought the rector a yearly income of £539 10s. 1d., a handsome sum in those days. The glebe land consisted of about 100 acres, and later, when his wife brought him the Rushford estate, Hayter George was owner of a fine stretch of land.

Mr. Clampitt was the other large landowner of the parish. In 1840 he owned Combe and Quintatown, while part of Middlecott belonged to his brother, Gabriel. In 1847 Nicholas bought Holy Street Manor from the Southmeads, along with their third share of the manors of Chagford and Collerew. After his death in 1869 Holy Street was bought by the Rev. Arthur Whipham, rector of Gidleigh and lord of the manor of that parish. After his death his son, Alfred Guy Whipham, sold his share of the manors of Chagford and Collerew to Thomas Taylor Coniam who already held the other two-thirds share, although Alfred remained at Holy Street.

The Coniams were settled at Waye Barton, but in 1826 there had been a fire there and this may be the reason why Thomas Taylor Coniam was living in Mill Street in 1857, if Waye was being rebuilt.

Of the other landowners, various members of the Ellis family had property at Week, Drewston, Stinial, Wolfeshall and Southill. The Hoopers held land at Lakeland, Higher Jurston, Great Week, Withecombe, Stinial, and some property in the village.

Whyddon Park was the property of Edward Seymour Bailey, but he did not live there.

Samuel Hunt was the surgeon, and, like the rector, his family were to hold that position in the parish until the end of the century.

The rector, the doctor, and the land-holding families were the stabilising forces in the community, but from outside came the forces of change. Communications were the key to those changes. Carrier services had been in operation from Exeter to London since the 17th century and in the 18th century several waggon services, taking goods and passengers, covered the same route. The mail coaches of the 18th century had set new records for fast communications with the capital.

Coach services with many other towns grew up, connecting smaller towns to a nationwide network, and when waggons were introduced into the Dartmoor villages and the roads were widened, some later turnpiked and tarmacked, by the 19th century carriages and coaches could be brought into Chagford. From the 1840s to the 1860s the ratepayers of Chagford were requested to attend meetings to decide the propriety of widening the Chagford lanes. In particular the lane from Sandy Park to Rushford and Chagford was re-routed to make it less steep. The deep cutting between Rushford Barton and Sandy Park was constructed and the road brought down beside the house, from its original position above the orchard. The way wardens, as in previous days, were responsible for the maintenance of the parish roads and, every year, tenders were taken for the upkeep of the tools used to repair the highways, an average figure of £3 a year.

The road from Rushford bridge to Crossways was also widened and among the specifications for this work is 'the top of the hedge shall be of good earth and planted with thorns', and later 'The gate now leading into Teign Meadow shall be removed to a point in the fence indicated by the owner and a stile shall be erected at the place where the gate now is, of good oak bars, 5in. in depth and 4in. in width'.

The following year the Chagford to Easton road was widened in four different places, near the opening to Crannafords, by the field called the Great Yews, and in two other places. Cross Park Hill was widened.

Over the following years the lanes were widened at Quintatown Hill, between Old Walls and Teigncombe, at Frenchbear, through Rushford Mill as far as Rushford bridge, at Thorn Hill, near Sand's Gate, between Corndon and Hurston, between Batworthy and Middlecott, and between Thorn and Yeo. Oat Hill Lane, leading to Meldon Common was widened, and also Singmoor Lane from Middlecott Cross to Batworthy.

In 1836 the Bovey Tracey to Okehampton road, through Moretonhampstead, was turnpiked. With the creation of a tarmac road through Easton and Sandy Park, road communication to Chagford took a leap forward and much of the subsequent widening and improving of the parish lanes included tarmac or metalling. It must have been at this stage that the normal route to Moretonhampstead became the Chagford to Easton lane, so joining the turnpike road at its nearest point, though some travellers to Moretonhampstead used to go from Easton to Cranbrook and so to Moretonhampstead. The turnpike road was not free, but the turnpike charges were not exhorbitant, and it was especially convenient for the woollen mill, which relied on efficient transport.

However important the new roads became, a more extraordinary form of transport had arrived—the railways. The Plymouth to Princetown railway was completed in 1823. In 1844 a main line railway was brought from Bristol to Exeter, and by 1849 the line had been extended to Plymouth, reaching Teignmouth in May 1846, and Newton Abbot by the end of that year. In 1851 a line was opened from Exeter to Crediton, and in 1871 Okehampton was joined to the Exeter to Barnstaple line. In 1866 Moretonhampstead was connected to Newton Abbot, and the railway was within six miles of Chagford. Plans were later made to bring the railway to Chagford itself, but the decline in the woollen industry made it seem less economic.

The year 1860 saw the first attempt to bring the railway to Chagford. It was to come from Dunsford, through the Teign Gorge, and would have puffed its way along the Teign until it met the factory buildings at Chagford bridge. This was its destination. From here another branch continued down the Teign past Holy Street to South Tawton and Okehampton. The railway to Chagford was proposed on four different occasions, but it never arrived.

The better-off members of the local community might now travel by coach or carriage to Moretonhampstead and by railway to Newton Abbot and Exeter. From Exeter, the Great Western Railway would carry them directly to the capital. A London gentleman might step on to the train at Paddington and arrive in Exeter within six hours. Such things would have been unthinkable only a generation previously, but it was inevitable that links of this kind should bring other innovations with them.

The driving force in the community from the time that he took over his father's position in 1852 was Hayter George. His wife was no less enthusiastic than her husband to improve conditions in the village. One of the first matters to be brought in hand was the town water supply. At that time the village was still supplied by an open stream that ran through the streets and was both supply and public drain. The advice of an engineer was taken, the stream was covered over, and a sewerage system laid. A good supply of pure water was provided to replace the 'Town Lake', which had supplied the open stream which was both supply and drain. There was a pump beside Ceylon House and another at the lower junction of the Square. Troughs still standing in the streets may suggest other pumps, where horses could be watered, and pails filled. There was an opening for dipping water in Mill Street. The woollen mill took an ample supply of water for washing and for power, as in medieval days, and the leats from New Street to the Mill Street site and the Old Mill Leat through Factory Cross provided the necessary water. Some of these water-courses are still visible, but much has either gone underground, or disappeared.

In 1869 a gas company was formed and gasworks were established on part of the woollen mill site. This provided gas lighting for the streets of the town, and was used to light some of the houses. Doubtless many people preferred to use their oil lamps as before, but dark night-time streets ceased to exist.

A more radical change occurred in 1891. Mr. G. H. Reed had moved to Chagford and established himselt at Teign View, a house he had built. Here he had large workshops where he kept his traction engine. He was by inclination a true Victorian inventor, spending his days in the investigation and invention of his many new machines. In 1891 an electric company was formed under his management, which took over the site of the woollen mill, which had recently closed down. The water power was used to generate electricity, which now replaced gas as a means of lighting.

An extract from the parish magazine of 1891 brings up an interesting point:

> There has been much talk lately about the electric light which it is proposed to introduce into Chagford. Mr. Reed has been showing off the light in the old factory which he has taken, and many people assembled on two occasions to see it. The question of conveying it underground, or overground by poles, has been considered at a meeting of the ratepayers of Chagford. Some were in favour of the wires being carried underground, and not overhead. It was pointed out that to insist upon this would practically defeat the scheme. On a show of hands being taken 25 voted for the wires being carried overground and 14 against. We hope that the electric light may find its way into Chagford, as there is such a excellent water power existing, it seems a pity not to use it. We wish the promoters all success.

Chagford became the first place west of London to light its streets by the use of electricity. The tumbling streams and rivers of the parish were, of course, ideal for this purpose, and both the mill at Yeo and that at Holy Street were later adapted for this purpose.

The woollen mill closed in 1848. A variety of circumstances made it uneconomic and production ceased. This lead to a decrease in population, for there was no longer the incentive of certain employment to bring people into the village and probably contributed to some of the younger people moving into the towns.

The 19th century saw a greater increase in building than previous centuries, especially in the town. Slate began to replace thatch, drills had started to be used on granite, giving craftsmen greater control and facility of working with that hard stone. The appearance of the village started to change.

Samuel Hunt built a house in Mill Street in 1841, and Nicholas Clampitt built one in the same street the following year. Addly House was built in 1856 by Mrs. Ellis.

Fire was a common hazard. In 1845 there were fires in Mill Street and in the Market Place at the houses of Mr. W. Hooper, Mr. G. Murch, and Mr. R. Stanbury. In 1855 another fire in the Market Place damaged the houses of Mr. J. Stone, Mr. W. Scott, Mrs. Maude, and Mrs. Harvey. Later that year there was a fire at the *Ring of Bells,* which in 1860 was actually burnt down.

These fires occasioned rebuilding or new building. Nor was it only the houses in the village that suffered from fire. Fernworthy farmhouse, then owned by Sir H. R. Ferguson Davie, was burnt down in 1855, and the following year Mr. J. Pitt's house at Underdown suffered a similar fate. Mr. Clampitt's stable at Combe caught fire in 1856. In the absence of fire engines and with so many thatched buildings, fires were terribly destructive, but in rebuilding the owners could take advantage of new materials, skills and styles. Of other houses built at this time, Cranley House went up in 1862, built by Mr. J. Hooper, Jnr., Brook House in 1864 by Mr. J. Collins, and Walland Hill in the same year by Mr. J. Hooper. In 1866 Mr. J. Collins built South-combe. That gentlemen were building houses on their several plots of land within the village, while already resident elsewhere shows another change in village life. New professions, occupations and types of residents created a demand for pleasant town houses, where only cottages had been required before.

A glance at the *Directories* for Devon in those years shows this more clearly. The number of builders, carpenters and ironmongers increased, as did drapers, tailors and shoemakers. In 1857 Miss Elizabeth Brock was a stay-maker, and there were several milliners.

Postal services had been in operation since 1824, but it was greatly improved by the advent of the railways. The mail was now brought down by train and a mail-cart took it to Moretonhampstead. In 1854 the mail-cart was extended to Chagford, and letters reached Chagford within eighteen hours of leaving London. By 1876 the electric telegraph was in operation in the post office. Robert Hole Thorn was the postmaster. In addition to the post office in Chagford, by 1882 there was also a wall letter-box at Easton, from which collections were made daily at 4.45 p.m.

The police force was a creation of Victorian times. In 1857 a police office of the county constabulary was established at Chagford, with William Bray as the policeman.

By the 1880s the Chagford coffee tavern was opened with Mrs. Jeffrey as its proprietor. James Bowden is described as agricultural implement maker, smith and ironmonger, situated at Vulcan iron works. Henry Hooper was auctioneer. William Painter was monumental mason. Henry Reed is described as engineer, millwright, machinist, threshing-machine and traction engine proprietor.

While these people may have fulfilled some of these functions in the past, they would not have described themselves in those terms. These are the marks of specialisation. By the end of the century we find Albert Hunt was not only surgeon, but also public vaccinator; Ernest Hooper was both architect and surveyor; and Charles Evans was chemist and druggist. A sub-branch of the Devon and Cornwall Banking Company opened on Tuesday between 2.30 p.m. and 5.00 p.m., managed by A. Gregory.

With the introduction of better water, of gas, and, finally, of electricity, Chagford had better facilities to offer to visitors. Largely at the instigation of Hayter George Hayter Hames it was put on the map as a pleasant place to visit. With the new means of transport came the concept of visiting salubrious areas of the countryside, and the gentry, along with writers and artists, were drawn to Chagford as a place from which they could enjoy the scenery of Dartmoor. The hotels and inns did a good trade and any number of boarding-houses were in business by the 1880s.

A bill from the early years of the century reads as follows:

THREE CROWNS INN
Kept by John Brock
*

Good Entertainment for Man and Horse
*

With the creation of the railways, fewer people needed entertainment for horses. A different mood appears in the inns, soon to be named hotels. The *Three Crowns* was a hotel by the 1880s, as were the *Globe* and the *King's Arms*. These all catered to the new visitors, along with the *Baker's Arms* and the *Ring of Bells*. The *Moor Park* hotel was built in 1869, originally called *Niner's* hotel, after its proprietress, Mrs. Isabella Niner. After the closure of the woollen mill the site of the drying house was later converted into the *Moorlands* hotel.

Apart from the number of boarding houses, several people offered the visitor comfortable furnished apartments and even one or two of the farmhouses provided accommodation.

A wine and spirits merchant appeared, situated in a shop now occupied by the National Westminster Bank. 'W. A. Gilbey, Wine & Spirits' ran the shop sign.

In the 1870s an omnibus service began. Twice daily from October to June and three times daily in the summer months the horse omnibus left the *Three Crowns* for Moretonhampstead, where the railway could convey the travellers to the sea or into town.

For the visitors the attraction was primarily the country air and wild scenery. London and the industrial towns were at this time smoggy and polluted, and for the first time there was a crying need to return to the cleanliness and peace of the countryside. It was a new need, but a pressing one. One Chagford man came into his own. James Perrot, who knew the moor and the rivers intimately, became the Dartmoor guide. He personally led people over the moor and ran a flourishing business hiring out every description of horse-drawn vehicle and arranging trips about the countryside. One of his advertisements for the shop he kept in the Square in Chagford, from which he ran his business, reads:

J. PERROTT & SON,
Square, Chagford.

Fishing Tackle Manufacturers and Guides to Dartmoor.

Over 50 years thoroughly acquainted with every object of interest on the Moor. Those desirous of investigating the Moor apply to the above.

*   *   *

SADDLE HORSES, PONIES, CARRIAGES of every description
at Moderate Charges.

*   *   *

Photographs of the Neighbourhood Supplied.

It was James Perrot who instituted the posting-box at Cranmere Pool. He would take visitors by horse vehicle to Teignhead Farm, whence they would walk the rest of the way, regaled by local anecdotes. At Cranmere Pool James Perrot built a small cairn, with a bottle in it, for visitors to place their visiting cards. A small book, housed in a tin case was added, for people to sign their names.

Apart from his profession as a guide, he was also a fisherman, selling flies and tackle to those who enjoyed angling. The streams and rivers of the area provided yet another source of amusement for those on holiday. Among Hayter George's papers are the records of the fishing licences he issued on his water at Rushford. A letter from a little later—in 1910—gives a good idea of the angler's enthusiasm:

Druid Arms,
Drewsteignton,
Devon
June 18th, 1910.

Dear Sir,
    Thank you not only for the permit but the cordiality accompanying it.
    I was out yesterday and was very surprised. I am not a speciliused 'carpist' but this should be the carp angler's paradise. The pool swarmed with them and I'm sure there must be monsters there. Something, which I tried hard to catch a glimpse of for a long time, broke me badly, and I was using salmon wire. There are no sea-serpents there I suppose! To say something wild, as well as feel so, is a 'little way' with us anglers. We landed four, the heaviest 6 lbs. I wonder if we might use the boat to take us round the banks? If we may, perhaps you would very kindly give me a card saying where the key of the house is procurable? At the same time it would be interesting to know what the record weight for this preserve has been. I can safely say, from what I've *seen*, that it is almost, if not *the* best carp water in England.
    Fishing only with paste we shall not be likely to catch your boy's 'rainbows'. May he have good sport amongst them; but I doubt if there is sufficient fresh water supply for them to endure there many years, so he had better hurry up and catch them. Spinning a minnow from a boat is the way we catch the big ones so that the little ones may live.
                Thanking you most kindly again,
                    I am, dear sir
                        Yours faithfully
                            J. Perryman.

    A fascination with history was just beginning. G. Waring Ormerod was active in the parish in this respect in the middle years of the 19th century and began the long task of investigating the parish's prehistoric remains. By profession a solicitor, this enthusiastic gentleman began an interest in Spinsters Rock, in stone circles, stone rows and other pre-Roman remains, that helped to attract the attention of visitors. It was he who helped to institute the parish magazines in the 1860s. Geology, pre-history, tin-mining, the early churchwarden's accounts and all the parish events leading up to his own time absorved his avid attention. When the Cromlech of Spinsters Rock collapsed in January 1862 he helped to have it raised to its original position. Indeed, he was very disappointed that only days previously he had been unable to photograph it, due to bad weather conditions. In the parish magazines he wrote all the information he could find on the history of the parish and published a small volume on this subject. As a result the attention of the visitors was drawn to many objects they might otherwise have never thought about; while antiquarians, that new breed of amateur scholar, were also drawn to the parish.

    Changes did not appear simply in the form of visitors. Life altered in many fundamentals. One of the most far-reaching of these came in the form of education. David George was schoolmaster in Chagford as early as 1659 and in the last years of the 18th century Mr. William Short came to Chagford as schoolmaster. In 1845 he was succeeded by his son, Mr. Caleb Short, who taught in Chagford until his death in 1879. His successor was George Smith, whose wife, Josephine, also taught the children. In 1853 Mrs. Hames opened an infants' school, and in 1860 the almshouse in New

Street was made a schoolroom. Miss Ann Gidley presided over about 85 infants, the infants' school being entirely supported by Mrs. Hames. Mr. Caleb Short now taught the boys in a room over the infants, his average number of scholars being seventy.

By the end of the century the numbers had greatly increased. The National School had an average attendance of 140 and the Infants of sixty-nine. The government had, by now, begun to make real provision for education; an extract from the parish magazine of 1891 discusses the matter in some detail:

> Sept. 1891 Schools.
> The Managers have decided to accept the Fee Grant of 10s per head, the amount paid by the Elementary Education Act, 1891. All scholars in future attending our schools between the age of 3 and 15 will be free. Before the reassembling of the Schools, due notice will be given to every ratepayer in the parish of this change. As hitherto it will be necessary that about £75 a year be provided by Voluntary Contributions, Offertories, Concerts etc. and as long as this can be done our parish will be exempt not only from 'School Fees' but 'School Rate'. In other parishes where School Boards exist, the amount over and above what Government pays will be obtained as in the past from the rates. In our adjoining parishes with School Boards, although free from School Fees as we are, the parishioners will still be called upon to pay the School Board Rate. The whole subject will be more fully dealt with in detail in the circular which will soon be in the hands of every ratepayer in Chagford.

In addition to schooling, which must have brought a tremendous change to the life of the children of the parish and to their families, a library and reading room was now opened. It was called the Church of England Temperance Reading Room and housed about 500 volumes. John Holmes was the curator. The reading room survived until the end of the century and was dissolved in 1907.

New forms of recreation came into being. In 1857 a Society of Chagford Archers was founded, in which ladies and gentlemen practised that graceful art. In 1859 there is record of a ploughing match at Chagford of the Chagford and Drewsteignton Agricultural Association and in 1861 the Archaeological Association visited Chagford.

Lectures became a feature. Mr. Bury gave a lecture on the honey bee, the Rev. W. Brown spoke on armour and in 1866 Mr. Ormerod's subject was mental cultivation. We can only speculate upon the audiences at these events and their appreciation of the topics chosen.

However, the most popular of new amusements must have been the Chagford Amateur Concerts, which occurred every year during the summer months. These raised funds for the schools and the reading room, but also became a feature of Chagford life. The accounts in the Parish magazines of these events give the flavour of the concerts very well.

> Parochial Concerts: Sept. 1893
> The Concerts which are generally given in Chagford at this time of the year have been very good, and we have had the pleasure of listening to an excellent programme of music on each occasion. This year we have had an unusual amount of talent in instrumental music, and in this we must mention some charming duets on the guitar and mandoline by the Misses McGavin. We have also been favoured by some delightful playing by Messrs. Hedgeland and Rowe, and Mrs. Stark's pianoforte playing was, as usual, much admired. Mrs. Morrison gave, as last year, some whistling solos which were evidently as much appreciated as ever. And amongst others who helped we must include the Misses Ralli, who, as young performers on the violin, acquitted themselves admirably. All who took part deserve the thanks of the audience, we are sure, for giving such pleasant evenings.

1870. The Third Philharmonic Concert of the season came off on the 15th ult. the programme was varied, and proved attractive as the room was somewhat crowded. Without entering into details of the performance, we may say that Sir H. Bishop's celebrated glee, 'The Fox jumped over the Parson's Gate', was admirably rendered by Mdlle. Koenig, Mrs. Earle, Mr. Vinnicombe, Mr. Stockdale and Mr. A. D. Hunt, the latter throwing much humour into the subject by his droll emphasis on the words 'a good fat hen, and away she goes'. The audience were evidently pleased with this, and it was rapturously encored. Miss Koenig won a similar compliment in an animated French song, 'The Nennella', which was finely sung, and displayed much masterly execution. A charming solo was played on the Zither by Herr Herkomer; the tone of this instrument was superb, and it fairly spoke to us; Herr Herkomer was recalled amidst general applause, and kindly treated us to another melody. Mr. Stockdale's comic song, 'The Trinklied', gained, also a well merited encore and the concert altogether was worthy of the reputation which our Philharmonic Society has gained.

At the conclusion of the performance, Captain Arkwright M.P., proposed a vote of thanks to the amateurs who had assisted, and spoke in flattering terms of their services: this was received with acclamation, and the Rev. H. G. Hames acknowledged the compliment on their behalf.

In addition to concerts and lectures, Penny Readings were begun:

1870. On the 23rd ult., W. Colebrooke Stockdale Esq., gave a dramatic Reading from Sheridan Knowle's comedy, 'The Hunchback'. The room was tastefully decorated on the occasion, and the proscenium dressed with ferns and festoons. The Chagford Orchestral Band was stationed on either side, and played selections of Offenbach's comic opera 'The Grand Duchess' between the acts. The reading was of a brilliant description, and elicited the loud and repeated plaudits of the assembled audience, which comprised most of the visitors staying in Chagford. At the conclusion the Rev. H. G. Hames moved a vote of thanks to the talented reader, remarking that his impersonation of the various characters in the play, and his power of declamation and passion, had afforded them a specimen of lofty genius in the mimic art; and after thanking him on behalf of the poor, among whom the net proceeds of the entertainment would be distributed, he expressed the hope that on no very distant date his accomplished friend would discover himself again on the platform before them, so beautifully and artistically adorned. The motion was carried by the acclamation, and Mr. Stockdale returned thanks.

This led to another reading, as the same magazine relates:

New School Room, Chagford—On Saturday evening, September 3rd, W, Colebrooke Stockdale Esq., had kindly consented to give a second Dramatic Recital from Shakespeare's celebrated comedy 'As You Like It', in aid of the improvements in the New School Room, which, on this occasion will be, for the first time, illuminated with gas. The Quadrille Band will play between the Acts. The Songs and Choruses incidental to the play will be rendered by a company of amateurs under the direction of Mr. E. M. Vinnicombe.

From May 1890, Penny Reading:

A very pleasant evening was spent on Easter Monday April 7th. A series of songs and readings was given in the Infants Schoolroom, the charge of admission being one penny. Mrs. Smith and Miss Jackson began by playing a piece on the piano, and songs were sung by Miss Ballamy, Mrs. Yeo, the Misses Mackenzie and the Rector. An amusing reading was given by Mr. Smith and an instructive one by Mr. Thomas Aggett. The evening came to an end by a comic song, sung by Mr. Benjamin Perrott, which greatly amused the audience, 'See me dance the Polka'. A vote of thanks should have been passed to Mr. Hayter-Hames for his kindness in lending the room and for his trouble in arranging the programme. As 250 people were present, in fact there was hardly standing room, it shows that an entertainment on Bank Holiday is appreciated. The proceeds were given for providing some new benches.

There was also the Sunday School Treat:

> Aug 1888. The Sunday School Treat will be held on Tuesday next, Sept 4th. It has been arranged to go to Dawlish. The children will meet at the National School at a quarter to nine punctually. A short service will be held in the Church at 9 a.m. and immediately afterwards the children, with their teachers, will start for Dawlish. Little children will not be taken unless someone has special charge of them. We hope that the day will be fine, that we may all have an enjoyable day. The offertory we may mention, throughout the day on August 26th was for the purpose of our treat, and we are very grateful for the liberal response that was made—it amounted to £11 2s 2d.

The parish was slowly absorbed into the mood of the times. The revolution in technology, new ideas in history, archaeology and natural history all filtered into Chagford. Yet these were matched by a greater strictness and fastidiousness in social life and most clearly in religion. The interior of the church was entirely restored in the second half of the century and the Rev. H. G. Hayter Hames was the force behind so many of the alterations, improvements and innovations of those years. As a 19th-century rector his responsibility for the souls of the parish was very broad and in no way confined to the church. The Church of England Temperance Society, the concerts and readings, schoolings and education were all in sharp contrast to the rural joviality of the previous century.

Church attendance had been for a thousand years a fundamental of the life of almost every member of the community, but now it took on a greater solemnity. Perhaps it would be true to say that now religion became not just a matter of the heart, but also of the mind, and close attention and participation were required. The old high-backed pews disappeared in favour of new ones from which it was possible to see and hear clearly. The string band was replaced by the beauty and grandeur of the organ. Many of the windows had stained glass erected in them, thus darkening the interior of the church. In 1870 a fund was started to raise money to light the church with gas light; later electricity was brought in.

Hayter George was a J.P. and his son Colville also held this position. In 1886 Hayter George died and since Colville had no desire to take holy orders, a new rector was appointed in the person of Gerald Ley. A new rectory was built on part of the glebe land, and the previous rectory became Chagford House.

The letter that Gerald Ley wrote is characteristic of the personality that Chagford was to know so well:

Chagford,
Newton Abbot

March 20th

My dear Sir,
  I have to thank you for your kind letter and the offer to me, as Trustee, of the living of Chagford. I have intimated to Mrs. Hayter Hames my acceptance of the same and I now write to tell you that I will gladly do so, thanking you very heartily in the matter. In accepting your kindness and the kindness of all the Hames family I can only say how pleased I am to be able to enter the parish as Rector at the express wish of him who for so many years had the charge of souls here, to whom I owe my gratitude but which I cannot now express, though this may be granted some day.

I beg them to accept the living of Chagford with many thanks and a deep sense of the great responsibility which will be laid upon me.

I am dear Sir
Very faithfully yours,
Gerald L. H. Ley.

The following year Gerald married Beatrice, the youngest of Hayter George and Constance's daughters, and they were both active throughout the parish and well-known by the parishioners. Of their two sons and three daughters, Cyril became a monk and Grace a nun, while Henry became organist of St. Martin-in-the-Fields and later of Eton College chapel. He was not only a fine musician, but composed for the organ himself and was an enchantingly eccentric character. Dora remained unmarried and spent the most of her life in Oxford. Geraldine married Mr. Herbert Adams and they live in Cambridge, but keep close links with Chagford.

Gerald Ley never tired in his duties to the parish. It was said that he could walk into any house in the village without knocking and he would be welcome. He was rector of the parish until 1911, when he died tragically young of consumption.

An intriguing church artefact came to light in the 19th century. In 1862 John Friball Macnamara visited the parish and heard of the old 'Roman altar'. He was able to find one John Squire who knew where it was buried and they dug it up together with a holy water stoup and some ancient glass, and left it standing in the churchyard. Its origins remain obscure. Authorities differ in dating it. It has been called the old high altar of the early church and equally a 16th-century tomb. There is no record of a high altar having been removed from the church in any of the old accounts; perhaps a tomb or a lesser altar are the more likely explanation.

The place that Hayter George had occupied in the parish was taken up by his son, Colville, and it was therefore with some excitement that the parish joined in the celebration of his marriage to Miss Violet Bradshaw of Powderham. The parish magazine gives a full account.

April 1897

The Wedding Day
The Wedding, which all the parish had been so greatly interested in, took place on February 24th. Joyous peals on the bells in the early morning proclaimed the event about to take place. The Choir and a few others started just before 9 a.m. and arrived in good time for the ceremony. St. Clement's Church, Powerham, was very prettily and simply decorated for the occasion. After a short practise of the music, the choir took their places whilst the congregation were assembling. At 12.30 with due regard to punctuality, the bride arrived and the marriage ceremony began. The Rector of Chagford officiated, in the absence of the Earl of Devon, Rector of Powderham, assisted by the Curate of Powderham. The service was fully choral, and well rendered by the choirs of Powderham and Chagford combined. After the service was concluded the bells were rung, but only a few peals, out of respect to the memory of the late Countess of Devon, whose death had taken place only a few days before. At the Castle a very large number of guests sat down to the wedding breakfast in the magnificent dining room. No speeches were made, but all present, and many others too, wished the bride and bridegroom all happiness and prosperity. At 3 p.m. the happy pair departed for London, on their way to France and Italy. The carriage was decorated with the usual adornments suitable to the occasion, but we have little doubt that these superfluous articles were taken off again before Exeter was reached.

In the evening the choir and bellringers had dinner at the Moor Park Hotel to which they were kindly invited by Mr. Hayter-Hames. The tenants were also provided for in the same hospitable manner at the Three Crowns. Nor were the Poor forgotten. All the parish received a good dinner from Chagford House. A dance in the school room followed and was kept up till 12.30, and we believe everybody thoroughly enjoyed themselves. We are sure that not only was this the case, but that everybody fully appreciated Mr. Hames' kindness, and that good wishes to the Squire of Chagford and his bride were unanimously felt, if not expressed, by every man, woman and child in Chagford.

In addition to the John Weekes Charity that provided education for poor children, there was also John Hooper's Charity which left the clear yearly sum of £5 to be distributed on New Year's Day to poor families who had not received any relief from the parish for one month preceding New Year's Day.

There was also the Church Lands Charity, the gift of an unknown benefactor, providing about £30 a year. Two thirds of this went to the rector and churchwarden and the remainder was administered by the trustees.

It was during the 19th century that the writer Charles Kingsley came to visit the parish. He was among the first of several well-known personalities to enjoy the countryside of the parish and use it as a base from which to explore Dartmoor. Extracts from his letters to his wife, written from the *Three Crowns*, follow here:

'I am quite in spirits at the notion of the Moor. It will give me continual excitement; it is quite new to me—and I am well enough now to walk in moderation.'
'Here I am at Chagford in a beautiful old mullioned and gabled 'perpendicular' Inn—granite and syenite everywhere—my windows looking out on the old Churchyard, and beyond, a wilderness of lovely hills and woods—two miles from the Moor—fresh air and health everywhere. I went up into the Moor yesterday, and killed a dish of fish.'
'September 4th. Starting out to fish to Drew's Teignton—the old Druid's sacred place, to see Logan Stones and cromlechs. Yesterday was the most charming solitary day I ever spent in my life—scenery more lovely than tongue can tell. It brought out of me the following bit of poetry, with many happy tears:

> I cannot tell what you say, green leaves,
>   I cannot tell what you say;
> But I know there is a spirit in you,
>   And a word in you this day.
> I cannot tell what you say, rosy rocks,
>   I cannot tell what you say;
> But I know there is a spirit in you,
>   And a word in you this day.
> I cannot tell what you say, brown streams,
>   I cannot tell what you say;
> But I know there is a spirit in you,
>   And a word in you this day.

Reply:
> O, rose is the colour of love and youth,
> And green is the colour of faith and truth
>   And brown of the fruitful clay.
> The earth is fruitful and faithful and young,
> And her bridal morn shall rise ere long,
> And you shall know what the rocks and streams
>   And the laughing green woods say!'

'Later. Got on the Teign about three miles up from Two Bridges and tracked it into the Moor. About two miles in the Moor I found myself to my delight in the ruins of an old British town, as yet, I fancy, unknown. The circular town wall, circular gardens, circular granite huts, about twenty feet in diameter, all traceable. All round was peat-bog, indicating the site of ancient forests. For you must know that of old, Dart Moor was a forest—its valleys filled with alder and hazel, its hillsides clothed with birch, oaks, and 'care', mountain ash. But these, like the Irish, were destroyed to drive out the Cymry, and also dwindled of their own accord, having exhausted the soil; and moreover, the scrub, furze, and heather which succeeded them, have been periodically burnt down for centuries, that grass for cattle may spring up. So that the hills are now covered with coarse pasture, or a peat soil, which wraps the hills around, and buries the granite rocks, and softens all the outlines till the Moor looks like an enormous alternation of chalk downs and peat bogs, only that the downs are strewn with huge granite stones and capped with 'tors', which cannot be described—only seen. I sketched two or three this afternoon for you.

Well, I got to Teign Head—through a boggy glen. Out of the river banks, which were deep peat, I got a piece of fossil birch bark for you. Then I climbed a vast anticlinal ridge, and seeing a great tor close by, I could not resist the temptation and went up. Oh! What a scene! A sea of mountains all around, and in the far east wooded glens, fertile meadows, twenty miles off—far—far—below; and here and there through the rich country some spur of granite hill peeped up, with its tor, like a huge ruined castle, on the top.

Then in the midst of a bog, on the top of the hill, I came on two splendid Druid circles, "The Grye Wethers", as I afterwards found out, five and thirty yards in diameter—stones about five feet above the bog—perhaps more still below it—evidently a sun temple in the heart of a great oak forest, now gone. I traced the bog round for miles, and the place was just one to be holy, being, I suppose one of the loftiest woods in the Moor. After that, all was down, down, over the lawn and through deep gorges, to the East Dart.

At Post Bridge, I meant to sleep, but found myself so lively that I walked on the four miles to this place—twenty miles about, of rough mountain, and got in as fresh as a bird. The day was burning bright, so I only killed a dozen or so of fish. Every valley has its beautiful clear stream, with myriad fish among great granite boulders. Today I walked over, after breakfast, to Cherry Brook, the best fishing on the Moor—the sharp easterly wind made the fish lie like stones—and down Cherry Brook and up Dart home, and I only killed seventeen. Then, after luncheon, I sallied to Wistman's (Wiseman's) Wood—the last remaining scrap of primeval forest. But I shall write all night to tell you all I saw and felt. I send you an oak leaf from the holy trees, and a bit of moss from them—as many mosses as leaves—poor old Britons! The grey moss is from the ruins of an old Cymry house near by—a Druid may have lived in it! The whortleberry is from the top of a wonderful rock three miles on, which I have sketched. Oh, such a place! I climbed to the top. I was alone with God and the hills—the Dart winding down a thousand feet below—I could only pray. And I felt impelled to kneel on the top of the rock—it seemed the true state to be in in any place so primeval—so aweful—which made one feel so indescribably little and puny. And I did pray—and the Lord's Prayer too—it seemed the only thing to express one's heart in. But I will tell you all at home! It is an infinite relief and rest to me to have seen even some little of the Moor. I was always from a child longing for it, and now, thank God, that is fulfilled. To-morrow I walk to Holne by Cator's Beam, i.e. over the highest mountain on the South Moor, from which all the South Devon streams rise. Sunday I spend at Holne, and Thursday home. It seems—sometimes a day, sometimes a year since I saw you. I shall bring you home several drawings and sketches, both of figures and of the Moor scenery. Kiss the darling babies for me.'

Living in Chagford at this time was another well-known local artist, William Morrish. His paintings of Dartmoor, executed during the 19th century, are well-known in Devon and treasured by lovers of the Moor. Born in Chagford, he lived here throughout his life and set up a picture gallery in the Square.

The weather, as always, was a source of consternation. In 1859 there was skating on Mr. Berry's fish pond and during several winters there are records of deep snow and people perishing in drifts. Ormerod says that in 1865 most of the ponies on Dartmoor died in the snow. In 1866 when the snow melted there were bad flood; half of Holy Street Bridge was washed away. In 1891 there was a really severe blizzard. Gale force winds brought heavy snow and created deep drifts. The wind snapped off trees and turned over iron seats and it was recorded that in some places, women and children were blown off their feet. The Plymouth railway line was blocked, a train running from Princetown to Plymouth was snowed up on the line, and several lives were lost at sea. Although these conditions did not last more than a few days, they were apparently severe enough to do considerable damage.

There was worse. In 1858, and in 1863, Ormerod records there were earthquakes around the area of Chagford, and in 1866 another slight shock was felt. None of these can have been much more than tremors, for there is no record of their causing damage.

By 1900 the outside world had penetrated Chagford's life and changed it. As Ormerod wrote in 1876, 'Those who remember the quaint old town, with its many thatched roofs and casement windows, may possibly look with some regret upon the alterations which have been made, but they are only parts of a series of Changes that are everywhere taking place.'

In the space of that one century almost every aspect of parish life had altered. Roads and railways, with their accompanying waggons, coaches, carriages and trains had become a feature of life. The streets were lit by electric light. The farms had threshing machines and mowing machines. There was now a bank, with bank holidays, an auctioneer, a chemist, a postmaster and a policeman.

There was a new rectory and a new rector. The interior of the church had been completely restored. For the children there was state education.

These were just the signs of a change that had occurred in the Englishman's view of his world. He had learned to understand many of the natural laws of the universe and he could harness them to his own ends. The theories of Charles Darwin described man himself as a part of those mechanistic laws. However revolutionary those theories were, they were filtering into every corner of life. People saw their world differently, they made it different and they began to see themselves in a new light.

The pace of life had altered, agriculture still tied Chagford to the changing patterns of the seasons, but something had been set in motion that was to explode into the extraordinary developments of the 20th century.

Chapter Fourteen

THE TWENTIETH CENTURY

THE FIRST HALF of the 20th century was dominated in Chagford, as it was throughout Europe, by the two World Wars. Queen Victoria died in 1901 and Chagford enjoyed for a short time the gentility of the Edwardian era. King Edward died in 1910 and only four years later, Europe found itself plunged into the darkness of hell.

Those first fourteen years of the 20th century were pleasant ones. The vigour and curiosity of the Victorians had brought a wide selection of new machinery, communications and pastimes to the village and there was the time to enjoy them.

But first, the death of one of England's great explorers, Henry Martin Stanley, brought very special visitors to Chagford.

In 1904 it was the wish of Lady Stanley to find some great monolith, 'fashioned by the Ages, tempered and coloured by Time, untouched by man', to mark the grave of one of England's greatest.

Lady Stanley suggested our searching Dartmoor to find such a stone, indicating the north-east corner as the most likely spot. Moretonhampstead, Chagford, Gidleigh, Wallabrook, Teigncombe, Batworthy, Castor, Frenchbeer, Thornworthy, Fernworthy, Hempstone and Grimspound were explored, and amid the thousands of stones few contained all that was essential to such a scheme. The river stones were rounded, smooth and pudding shape; those on Dartmoor irregular, and many much too massive; those most likely and most suitable were the most inaccessible, for this wild waste had few tracks and no roads upon which such a load can be conveyed.

It became evident that more attention should be given to the moorland farms which have roads leading into the border towns. Our mission being explained, the owners and tenants showed the keenest interest, and many were the offers of stones for Stanley's memorial. After several days thus employed, a large granite monolith was discovered on Frenchbeer farm which seemed at once to impress itself as being 'the stone', and upon careful examination it was found to contain all that was essential, its extreme length being 12 ft., width varying 4 ft., 2 ft., to 2 ft. 6 ins. in thickness. It was in a recumbent position, forming part of a fence on the road side; three faces had been fully exposed for many years.

The owner, Robert Stark Esq., and the tenant Mr. George Mortimer, most cheerfully gave their consent to its removal, only stipulating that a brass plate should be fixed to a smaller stone stating that from the spot was removed the stone which now stands at the head of Stanley's grave. The five smaller stones which form the boundary of this simple enclosure were found in the immediate neighbourhood. These moorland stones are for the greater part recumbent. The few which remain today were raised as memorials to chieftains; others form circles, huts, and avenues, and remain to us the silent witnesses of a race of whose history we know so little. Whatever their past history may be, it seems fitting that one should be raised in our time to this great African leader. It has now a definite work to do, and for ages yet to come will bear the name of that great son to whom the wilds of Dartmoor were as nothing compared with that vast continent which none knew better than he, and whose name will live, not by this memorial, but as one of the great pioneers of Christianity, Civilisation and Hope to that dark land. The removal of these stones from Dartmoor to Pirbright was not a matter of everyday occurrence, and again the Devonshire people showed their interest. As the stone passed through Chagford and other places snapshots were taken as mementoes of its progress. The Devonshire roads being steep and difficult, it was found necessary to employ a traction engine and waggon to convey it to the railway at Morehampstead. After much labour the great stone, weighing upwards of six tons, now stands in Pirbright churchyard, imperishable as the name cut deep into its face.

The words of the inscription were chosen by Lady Stanley. She wrote 'I desire simply his name, Henry Morton Stanley, beneath is his great African name, Bula Matari—the Rock Breaker. For epitaph, the single word Africa, and above all, the emblem and assurance of life everlasting—the Cross of Christ'.

Despite this brief association with the exploration of Africa, the early years of the 20th century in Chagford were years of peace and gentility. A cottage garden show was already in existence by 1905 and a carnival at least by 1912. In 1908 a golf course was opened so that 'we may be able to supply our numerous visitors with the means of playing this fascinating game'. Perhaps not all the population were in favour, for in announcing the opening of the links on Meldon, the parish magazine adds, 'If there are

Fig. 6. Chagford Square from Mill Street (line drawing by W.C. Matthews from photograph)

any who fancy that we do not need an introduction of this sort, experience, we believe, of the successful issue of the game as a pastime for many who come here, will quickly show that what is proposed to start on Whit Monday will be a benefit to Chagford and the surrounding district'.

The markets and fairs still happened regularly, although when they were let to Mr. S. North in 1909 the income was beginning to fall off. Doubtless the increased service of the Chagford shops and the speed with which the population could reach larger centres accounted for this.

Chagford now had a fire brigade, who were active in putting out a fire in two cottages near Jurston in 1906, but who, despite their best efforts, were unable to prevent the almost total destruction of Rushford Barton in 1913.

There was also a parish nurse. In 1907 Mrs. Anderson had been parish nurse for 16 years, but left to visit her son and daughter-in-law in Chicago. In her absence the Parish Nurse Fund secured the services of Miss Yardley, who belonged to Chagford, but had trained in London. Such travelling would have been unthinkable when Queen Victoria came to the throne.

It was in 1907 that the Chagford Reading Room came to an end. It had got into financial difficulties and despite attempts to revive it, the finances were not forthcoming. It closed in June and the books were sold.

1913 saw the introduction of two new institutions into Chagford, the Boy Scouts and the Mothers' Union. The Mothers' Union had first been suggested three years earlier, but there was some delay in getting a branch started. Gerald Ley wrote, 'After a little time we hope to make a beginning, but that which, under the providence of God and the leading of the Holy Spirit is to succeed needs careful and close consideration'. There could be a suggestion here that a Union of Women is a rather worrying concept, but the need for deliberation might have been on other grounds.

The Boy Scouts began in 1913, the first scoutmaster being the Rev. E. Barker, who was then assistant curate of the parish. The institution seemed popular from the start and was to play an important role in various aspects of work to support the war when it broke out the following year.

1911 was a sad year for the parish, for it saw the death of Gerald Ley, who had been their rector since the death of Hayter George Hayter Hames in 1886. Gerald Ley had been a true shepherd to his flock and his death from tuberculosis at the age of 57 was a severe blow to the parish. The living was filled by Hubert Studdy, at the introduction of Colville Hayter-Hames, whose nephew he was. Because of the family connection—Reverend Studdy's mother was Colville's sister—he was already familiar to the parish, which made the transition a great deal easier.

The Parish Magazine, May 1913:

The Belfrey—An Appeal

The state of the belfry is causing considerable anxiety, and will require much attention in the near future. Messrs. W. Aggett & Son, a firm famous in Devon and beyond, have drawn up a most reasonable estimate for the work needed. In their report they mention that in the year 1553 an inventory of Church goods was taken, when there were five bells in the Tower. Thomas Bilbie, of Cullompton, in 1766, recast six bells, when Joshua Hayter was Rector. Two bells were added in 1877 to make a peal of eight. 'The bells at present are in a bad condition, the supporting old oak beams are rotten at the ends that rest on the corbel. The bell frames are worn out. Some of the timbers have been cut about to make room for the bells to swing. The frames are sunk out of level, making the manipulation very hard work in peal-ringing. The present peal of eight are discordant, and some are of bad tone. The approximate weight according to measurement is about 3½ tons. This is quite sufficient when recast to make a good peal, and if tuned on Canon Simson's 5-tone principle, and sand-blasted, it will be a fine musical peal.'

500 guineas were required and a Fund was started to raise this money. In August of the same year a Fancy Fair was held to raise funds and by September the parish had found £620 towards the work. Events at the Fair included hoopla, weight-guessing, photography, sketches, mother goose, skittles, an exhibition of a model Japanese village, an aerial glide, a performance by the Chagford Band and by the handbell ringers, a selection of concerts by various young ladies and, later in the day, dancing on the lawn. By the end of 1913 work on the bells and on the tower was in hand.

1913 took from the parish another well-loved face, that of Beatrice Ley, who survived her husband by only 18 months. Hubert Studdy says of her, 'In her parish work, among her friends outside, as well as within the family circle the key note of Mrs. Ley's life was sympathy. She was full of that spirit of love which made it natural to her to rejoice with them that do rejoice and to weep with those that weep. She was a good listener, and, as such, she gained a wonderful knowledge of her people, of their troubles, trials and temptations. Many in after years will realize the influence for good which they received from that kind friend, who has been well described as the "Mother of the people".'

The stream of visitors to Chagford that had begun in Victorian times showed no sign of decrease. The hotels and boarding houses were busy and the rector was often subject to requests for information on places to stay within the parish. Among these visitors was the painter W. R. Sickert, who visited Chagford during the spring or early summer of 1915 and painted several scenes in and around the village. His subjects include Chagford Churchyard, Rushford Mill, the Post Office and 'The Blasted Tree', of which he wrote in a letter 'The subject was certainly a beautiful one . . . the rooks in the blasted tree in front. If only the painting could give a tenth of the charm of that quiet village'.

Sickert stayed at Teign View, where Mr. Reed let rooms. At about the same time as the painter's visit, a writer stayed there. Eden Phillpotts had been in Chagford before. His *Children of the Mist* was set around Rushford Mill and describes the parish scenery and many of its characters.

Easton Court was to receive a visit from Evelyn Waugh, who is said to have written part of *Vile Bodies* there.

In 1893 a little girl was born in Paris, little of whose life was spent in Chagford, yet who belongs to its history. Freya Stark was the daughter of Robert and Flora Stark. Freya's parents were cousins and their family had been in Devon for 200 years, but Robert had grown up in Torquay and knew and loved Dartmoor, while Flora had grown up in Italy and found the Dartmoor climate intolerable. In the earlier years of their marriage and while their two daughters were young, they lived in seven, and actually built four, houses in the area. Robert Stark had a gift for designing and laying out gardens. He designed and built Scorhill House at Gidleigh, owned Yelfords and designed and built Ford Park and rebuilt Frenchbeer. Flora, however, returned to Italy with her daughters, where Freya spent most of her young life. After the First World War she became an accomplished scholar of Arabic and travelled widely, writing many accounts of her travels. Now 87, she lives in Italy, but still returns to Chagford, to which she feels she most particularly belongs.

The early months of 1914 saw the beginning of the work on the church tower and the newly recast bells were hung. Messrs. Taylor & Son of Loughborough recast the bells, while Messrs. Aggett & Son of Chagford, whose premises were at the lower end of the Square, opposite the Forge, made the new frame for them and rehung them. The belfry floor had to be renovated and in the course of the work an ancient cross was discovered, which was to be preserved in the church. The work was completed by the end of the year and in January 1915 a service was held for the Blessing of the Bells.

It was in the late summer of that year that Miss Ethel Lega-Weekes, with the co-operation of Frank Osborne, began the task of translating the early churchwarden's accounts. An ancient manuscript in late medieval Latin, with frequently damaged pages, did not deter them from this labour of love, which was to occupy over a quarter of a century.

More tragic news came in August 1914 with the outbreak of the First World War. Hubert Studdy's monthly letter to the parishioners, written on 27th August 1914, gives a clear indication of the feeling of those days.

My dear People,

In this grave time of war, the greatest and most calamitous in the world's history, my duty is two-fold. First I urge all those who are in anxiety, trouble, or sorrow to make their Church at all times and at any hour their meeting place with God. Its doors are always open by day. You can therefore get away from the noise and bustle of the world into the quiet home, where you may better realize God's closeness and His care. There you will gain that peace which the world cannot give. Secondly, while our brave soldiers and sailors are doing all they can for us, it behoves us untiringly to do all we can for them. It would be a serious day for your home if our fighters grew slack and gave up heart. We depend on them to continue their magnificent zeal unfalteringly. They depend on us to continue prayer for them unfalteringly. As long then as this war lasts the Intercession Services on Wednesday evenings at 8.30 and on Thursdays after Evensong, will continue. Prove your Patriotism by your persistent prayers and Intercessions. Crowd to Church. You can do so much for those you love, and those you honour. Mountains of danger, mountains of calamity can be, nay, shall be removed by prayer. Forsake not the assembling of yourselves together. God will hear, God will answer. In the name of God, in the name of England's brave sons, and in the name of England's dear Mothers, I call on you to untiring intercession, unabated prayer. Do not weaken the ranks of prayer by dropping out of your place. Your country, your soldiers, your sons need you.

Your faithful servant in Christ Jesus,
Hubert C. Studdy.

The following years were to be dominated by the efforts and the tragedies of the war. Services of intercession were held twice weekly. Wool was collected so that the schoolgirls could knit socks for the soldiers. A convalescent home was run at Furlong which provided for the care of wounded soldiers, who were, in the early years of the war, predominantly Belgian. A Refugee Committee was formed and Mrs. Lloyd Hill's house adjoining Moorlands and Mrs. Stanford Perrot's house at 3 Fernleigh were engaged at a nominal rent to provide homes for refugees. Mrs. Drake at Collina took in a small family of refugees and Mrs. George Smith offered to take an orphan.

Early in January 1915 an egg collection was begun to provide eggs for the wounded. The collection and dispatch of these was largely arranged by the Boy Scouts.

Colville Hayter-Hames was given the job of buying local horses for the army. The following letter from C. H. Fulford shows the problems involved in providing for the war and for those at home.

Fulford,
Dunsford,
Exeter.

8 August 1914

My dear Col,

Frank, who is working at the board of Agriculture looking after food supplies writes that he is surprised to hear that so many horses are being taken from the farms for Army requirements, as he says that it was clearly understood that farm horses were to be left till the Harvest was in and he asks me to bring the matter before Captain Morrison Bell as M.P. so that he may ask a question about it in the House. I see however that he is called out and also I read the enclosed questions and answers in the House on this subject.

I don't wish to convey the idea that the farmers are complaining about this, on the contrary they are I think, extremely patriotic in the matter, but as Frank points out the extreme importance of getting the Harvest in, it is a question whether it is expedient so to denude the farms of horses at the moment that the Harvest may be seriously checked, and tho' I understand that the farmers can afford with but slight inconvenience to part with the horses which have been taken up to the present, I believe that a further call on horses is contemplated which may seriously interfere with Harvest operations.

You will forgive me for bothering you when you are so busy, but as Morrison Bell is away I thought it more to the point to write to you than to him.

With kind regards
Yrs. very sincerely
C. H. Fulford.

Farm work must have become very hard, for many of the younger men had left for the war. Twenty-seven young men from Chagford were in the territorials by the end of 1914, yet in May 1915 a recruiting tour secured only one recruit in Chagford, though several men were eligible. The parish magazine says that 'on all sides Chagford is pointed at as the most unpatriotic town in the district'.

The criticism is too strong. By 1918, 13 young men from Chagford's families had lost their lives, and three more had been seriously wounded. At first the deaths were intermittent, until the later years of the war began to take their toll and the tragic news came in all too rapidly.

The effort of the parish to contribute seems enormous. Prayers for the soldiers and for peace were one of the strongest weapons and the rector himself put every effort into the services of intercession and the morale of the community. Clothes and food were contributed to the soldiers and to the wounded. There were collections for Church Army Huts and for the Red Cross Society, there were collections of vegetables for the Fleet.

In 1916 the lovely new bells, along with the Church clock, had to remain silent after dark to conform with the Defence of the Realm regulations.

Mr. Barker, the assistant curate, offered himself as a volunteer, but was not needed. Later in the war he did join the army and was killed in 1918.

Hubert Studdy gave up the living of Chagford in 1916 and moved to Cockington, while the vicar of that parish, the Rev. T. Walters, came to Chagford. Only the following year Mr. Walters became an army chaplain and from then until he returned at the end of the war he wrote monthly letters to the parish from his post in France, with a devotion that seems typical of him. Despite his work at the front he remembered his parishioners and affairs at home in detail, and about which he often wrote.

A War Memorial Fund was begun in 1918 and an appeal put out in the parish. At last in November, the war came to an end. Mr. Walters returned home in May 1918 and was in his own parish to conduct the Service of thanksgiving when the news of the Armistice came through. Mrs. Critchley-Salmonson of Holy Street presented the old Chagford Cross, which had moved from the Square to Holy Street, to the parish as a memorial to the men of the parish who had fallen in the war. The churchyard was enlarged at the end of 1918, when Mr. Thomas Amery gave the church the additional lane and the memorial cross was finally erected within the new part of the churchyard. In addition, the list of those killed in the war was carved in the oak panelling of the lady chapel and an altar erected in their memory.

The war had finally reached its end. While the country began the work of 'national reconstruction' and the world tried to regain its sanity, a feeling of exhaustion seems to be felt in Chagford. After the horror and tension of those years, people were fundamentally tired.

The years from 1918–1939 seem years of quiet progress. The events in Europe receded for a time and the parish activities took up where they had left off. There was the rectory garden fete and amateur theatricals. The Boy Scouts and the Girl Guides, who had come into being during the War, were active. The Women's Institute was formed in Chagford.

The Carnival reappeared as an annual event and with the building of the swimming pool there was a yearly swimming gala.

The death of Noel Hayter-Hames in 1925 was a tragic blow to his family. Their memorial to him was erected in the church in the form of the lovely carved chancel screen. In 1928 his father, Colville Hayter-Hames, died and another long-familiar face disappeared from the parish. Within the church the pulpit was erected in his memory and dedicated in January 1930.

In 1922 the Rev. T. Bell Salter became rector of Chagford and occupied the living until his death in 1931. The Rev. W. Holmes took up the living. At the School Mr. Bennet was headmaster throughout these years. In 1936 the secondary school was opened with Mr. Jewells as headmaster and a new era began for education in Chagford.

Cars were by now a feature of Chagford life. A photograph of the first car to visit Chagford House was taken in 1917, but this must have been a rare occasion. It was only between the wars that cars gradually became more common and the use of horses finally began to fall off. Working horses survived longer on the farms, where they were not replaced by tractors until the 1930s. With a typical feeling for horses, an intriguing fund was raised in 1933 to buy back war horses from the Egyptians, give them a week's good feed and care, before destroying them with the humane killer. Chagford raised £22 2s 6d.

A happy occasion for Chagford was the wedding of Gerald and Beatrice Ley's eldest daughter Geraldine to Herbert Adams. 'All Chagford seemed to be there, to say nothing of the many friends from all parts of the county.' Geraldine's brother, Dr. Henry Ley, presided at the organ and the parish were given once more an opportunity to express their deep affection for the Ley family. 'The reception was held at the Rectory, the house where Miss Ley was the first baby to be born and from which she went forth as the first bride.'

1930 brought the death of Mr. Reed, whose technological skills had so assisted Chagford in the introduction of electric light, not to mention his wonderful traction engines. Mr. Reed had built Teign View, where he lived until the end of his life. His daughter, Emily, married Mr. Bartlett, who worked with Mr. Reed in the electricity company. It was their daughter, Winifred, who married Frank Osborne in 1920 and, now living at Bellacouch, is responsible for having encouraged the present author to write this history of Chagford.

In 1931 Mr. Bell Salter's death brought the Rev. Walter Holmes to Chagford until that gentleman's death in 1938, when the Rev. Charles Chadwick was introduced to the living. Since the death of Colville Hayter-Hames in 1928, his son, George, had been patron of the living and had taken up the responsibilities to the parish which his father had previously fulfilled.

Colville Hayter-Hames and Thomas Amery had been churchwardens together for many years and subsequently George Hayter-Hames and Charles Amery occupied the same positions in the community.

The Jubilee of King George was duly celebrated in Chagford in 1935, the programme of events being:

10.15 a.m.	Peal of Bells.
10.45 a.m.	Parade of ex-Service Men.
11.00 a.m.	United Thanksgiving Service in Church.
12.30 p.m.	Dinner for older people in Assembly Rooms, arranged by Women's Institute.
2.00 p.m.	Sports for all in the Moor Park Field.
6.00 p.m.	Children's Tea in the Senior School. Arranged by Women's Section, British Legion.
9.00 p.m.	Dance, Assembly Rooms.

The Jubilee provided the name for a new Chagford project, the building of a village hall. The Jubilee Hall was first discussed in 1935 and completed early in 1938.

A fundamental change in the landscape occurred with the creation of Fernworthy Reservoir. The towns of the south coast created a growing demand for water supplies and in 1927 Torquay built an intake works just below Fernworthy Farm to pipe water directly to their Frenchford Reservoir. It was not enough and in 1934 they obtained powers to construct a dam at Fernworthy. The afforestation of the area had already begun, for the farm was abandoned by the early years of the century and bought by the Duchy of Cornwall in 1917 to begin the planting of trees.

The Fernworthy dam was the last granite faced dam to be built on Dartmoor. In damming the South Teign and by virtue of the stands of conifers the ancient opening from Chagford to the higher slopes of Dartmoor was closed over. The work on the dam began in 1936, but a terrific thunderstorm in August 1938 brought 3½ ins. of rain in the area in 8 hours and the works were both flooded and silted up. The outbreak of war created further difficulties and the project was not completed until 1942, the lake formed covering 76 acres.

Fig. 7.   Teign Head, Chagford (from an etching by Samuel Prout)

Teign Head Farm was finally cut off from the lower valleys and has fallen into ruins. The creation of the Dartmoor National Park in 1949 put some restrictions on the further afforestation of the moor, but it is impossible that the forseeable future will remove that great shadow of trees where once the livestock of the village approached the open waste.

Corn milling ended in Chagford by 1917, when Sandy Park Mill ceased to grind corn. The steam roller mills in Plymouth and Exeter took over this ancient function and Chagford ceased to eat bread ground from its own corn.

Farming throughout the 20th century has become more specialised and more mechanised. The trend away from arable farming continued with the exception of the period of the First World War, when grain made a temporary comeback. Farmhouse fare, with its wide range of home produced foods, has gradually disappeared. The production of the farm slowly became a few large scale items for the general markets and even the traditional Devonshire cream is now only a feature of a few of the parish's farms.

Tractors were slowly introduced in the years between the wars, but became more prevalent when the pressures of the war effort and the lack of young men on the farms made machinery more necessary.

The telephone slowly became an accepted feature of life in those years. In the 1920s several of the parish businesses and some of the private houses took on this innovation. An advertisement in the parish magazine for 1926 announces, 'Get it at

Webber's: anything and everything for the house, garden, garage, stable, farm. Phone —one-three, Chagford'. Incidentally, Webber's sold wireless sets at this time.

The first meeting of the British Legion in Chagford occurred in October 1931 and another parish institution began.

Some land near Rushford Mill was given by George Hayter-Hames and the swimming pool was completed in 1936.

Sunday School treats had been a feature of the parish ever since Victorian times. The children were generally consulted and seem to have shown a preference for excursions to the sea. The school children gave concerts, and had sports days. On Empire Day they performed pageants and sang patriotic songs. There were evening classes organised by the Workers Educational Association in such subjects as cookery, first aid, and ambulance, orchard pruning and dairy farming.

In 1931, on Armistice Sunday, part of the plaster of the church roof collapsed and subsequent investigation proved that the roof had death watch beetle. A fund was begun to raise money to replace the damaged woodwork and treat the roof to destroy the beetle.

Parish life was continuing smoothly; the children did well at school, the church was carefully maintained, farming was prosperous and every year the harvest was celebrated in the harvest festival. Only murmurs from abroad disturbed the peace of Chagford minds.

Those who hoped that conflict in Europe could be averted were to be tragically disappointed. In August 1939 a new outbreak of hostilities began the Second World War. All the struggle and effort of 1914–1918 began again, but in a new and more modern form. The horror of the trenches was not to be repeated, but the air raids and the destruction of Plymouth and much of Exeter brought the war all too close to home.

In October 1939 there was an 'unprecedented raising of the income tax to 7/6d in the pound', which made the war effort only too clear to everyone. The saving of waste paper, the presence of children evacuees, a Chagford Spitfire Fund and the creation of mobile canteens by the British Legion to aid the bombed towns were all efforts by those remaining at home to help the war effort in every way.

The war was not entirely unexpected. In the crisis of 1938, preparations were begun. From the parish magazine there is the following note in October 1938:

A.R.P. NOTES

During the recent crisis the census of the Chagford population was completed and was found to consist of 642 men, 713 women, 176 children between the ages of 3 and 14, and 48 infants—a total of 1,579, excluding visitors in hotels and boarding-houses, but including men working at Fernworthy and their families in some cases.

The crisis showed how very important it is to have everything organised in advance for such an emergency. Though Chagford was more prepared than many places much still remains to be done. The Wardens have now all completed their training, and each Warden has been instructed to let each householder know that he or she is responsible for the inmates of that particular house. Each Warden, too, has been instructed to report the number of bed and sitting-rooms in each house. This information is required in the interests of the householders themselves, in order that, in the event of a war, they may not be subjected to the same amount of inconvenience as were the people in towns and villages nearer London.

There is a shifting population of lodgers and domestic servants and in order to keep the records up to date, the Head Warden would be very grateful if residents would report changes in their households either to their own Warden or in a note addressed to 'Head Warden, A.R.P. Headquarters, Three Crowns Hotel'.

The Second World War came so close to home. In 1941 a War Damage Insurance Scheme was begun to insure against the destruction of parish churches by bombing. A clothing collection in aid of Plymouth Relief, the work of the air raid wardens, the Devon emergency land workers scheme and in 1942 the Exeter Air Raid Distress Fund all showed how near the war had come.

There were continuing pleas for money, energy and goods. A fruit preservation scheme, for food was scarce, first aid courses, the Soldiers, Sailors and Airmen's Families Association Flag Day, the Red Cross and Order of St. John Fund, the call for fire fighters, Christmas presents for the forces and finally the stationing of troops in Chagford all took their toll on a parish, like every other, depleted of its menfolk, hard pressed to support itself, and aware in some way of the presence of an evil and violence in the world that must be overcome.

To make matters worse the church heating system broke down and church services in the winters became a cold affair. Due to restrictions the church bells became silent and it was only in 1944 that they were heard again.

Mr. Chadwick, who had only been in Chagford since 1939, took on, with the living, the responsibility of maintaining hope and stability through the war years.

George Hayter-Hames was now chairman of the Devon War Agricultural Committee, working to keep farm production at the necessary level. These were the days of the women's land army, since so many of the men were gone.

For those unable, by virtue of age or health, to join the army there was the Home Guard. The fact that air raids and the threat of invasion penetrated the country so deeply made it vitally important to provide some form of defence for those left at home. While there can be no doubt that the Home Guard did a marvellous job, they provided something far more important, fun and laughter.

By 1944 there was every hope of a victory for the Allies and spirits began to rise. In June 1945 the war in Europe was finally over and the church bells could ring again in peace, joy and safety.

National recovery took time. Rationing continued for some years, there were scarcities and shortages, but the fear had gone and as the second half of the century began, prosperity increased.

Technology, mechanisation, communications and wealth have all accelerated since the end of the Second World War. People come and go at a rate that would leave James Perrot breathless; perhaps it makes his grandson, Dick, now in his eighties, quite breathless, too. The tourist industry shows this feature all too clearly. It has grown out of all proportion since the end of the last war and sometimes threatens completely to stifle local life.

There has been a considerable increase in new building in the town and around the parish. Where it provides homes for residents it must be welcomed, but there is always the danger, in a society of such rapid travel and communications, that the owners of some of the new houses, and indeed of the old, do not become part of the parish. This is the feature that is slowly destroying village and community life throughout England.

Yet the village has been the home and greater family of individuals since the very earliest times we know, and there is no certainty that individuals are capable of surviving without such a focus.

The population fell consistently from 1871 to 1971 and has not reached its 1831 total again.

Population

1801: 1,115	1891: 1,460
1811: 1,197	1901: 1,397
1821: 1,503	1911: 1,548
1831: 1,868	1921: 1,715
1841: 1,836	1931: 1,584
1851: 1,557	1941: No census
1861: 1,379	1951: 1,589
1871: 1,530	1961: 1,346
1881: 1,450	1971: 1,250

The parish has become increasingly absorbed by the mechanisms of the modern world. Our water comes from the Meldon reservoir, near Okehampton, although the stand pipes are still Chagford water.

The ancient jurisdiction of the manor courts and of the churchwardens has evolved into the Parochial Church Council and the Parish Council, which began in 1895, with Hayter George as its first chairman, and Alf Jeffry, clerk. The duty of the waywardens now passes to the County Council and the roads and bridges are no longer kept up by Chagford men.

Farming has become increasingly mechanised, yet Chagford is lucky that so many of her farming families remain in their respective farms, generation by generation, for these have been for so long the backbone of parish life. The continuity of families among the farms gives Chagford life a stability it could never otherwise have.

Education has gone through an upheaval with the creation of the comprehensive school in Okehampton. The secondary school has become the primary school and everyone of secondary school age goes, by bus, to Okehampton every day.

A pony sale is held annually in October. Markets for cattle are held on the first Tuesday of March, April, June, August and November. Sheep markets are held on the second Monday in August and the first and fourth Mondays in September.

The Chagford Show, the carnival, the church fete and any number of charitable organisations continue their untiring work in the parish.

The church continues, ageless and serene, at the centre of village life. Christmas, Easter and harvest festival still pay tribute to the turning seasons. The church roof needs re-leading, as it always did. The church house needs new thatch.

To one walking across Padley Common, the bashing of hammers in New Street suggests prosperity and increase. Doubtless there are the same old joys, terrors, misunderstandings and skull-duggery there always was. Now we are cloaked in modern times.

The silent hills are testament to ancient men, now long gone from them. I often wonder about those ancient men; in Dartmoor's misty waste and in the valleys, among the tangled trees; hoping that the roots that they put down in this most lovely corner of the fruitful earth may flourish and grow, and that not only the people, but the many creatures and growing things, the tumbling streams and breathless moorland slopes may continue in their ancient wild beauty.

EPILOGUE

Spoken by one of the School Boys

At the conclusion of the Grand Amateur Concerts given at Chagford
on July 22nd, 1861, in aid of the new School Room.

[*Published by request.*]

Ye men of worth who long for Chagford's fame,
Ye ladies fair who smile on Chagford's name,
Accept from Chagford's sons their homage true,
Their grateful thanks for this your presence due.

We hail a day thus dignified by fate
To gain the favour of the good and great,
To see our schools permitted thus to share
Your names, *your* patronage, *your* fost'ring care.

This is a day with joy and gladness crowned,
With instrumental and with vocal sound,
With sounds long to be cherished when we part,
In fond remembrance of your skill and art.

This School! its future greatness who can tell?
Its present well-earned fame it may excel,
May boast of names of celebrated praise,
Like those I could recount of former days.

Some Berkeley, some Godolphin, sad to tell,
(So chronicled by Clarendon) who fell
In mortal combat at that time-worn gate
Where Chudleigh now for guests is seen to wait.

Some Wybery, some Whiddon, stern and just,
Who lies in marbled state and sculptured dust
In our old church; a church now known to share
A people's homage and a pastor's care.

Some Coniam and some Clampitt, men of praise,
Manorial Lords in past as present days,;
All glad to prove themselves good men and true,;
Some Rector Hames—some Hayter Bishop too.

Such be our hopes that this our school shall be,
Of greatness, love, and truth, the nursery
For teacher's fame; not *Short* of his great name
Who gives our school its honour and its fame.

These schools, this people, and this parish all,
Long may they last, and flourish great and small,
And from Okehampton down to Newton tell
A lesson which they cannot learn too well.

Accept now Ladies fair our thanks most true,
And all kind friends our thanks are due to you,
For instrumental music echoing round,
But most of all those charms of *vocal* sound.

BIBLIOGRAPHY

Transactions of the Devonshire Association.
Perkins, *Geology Explained: Dartmoor and the Tamar Valley.*
Worth, *Dartmoor.*
Thom, *Megalithic Sites in Britain.*
Robert Graves, *The White Goddess.*
Fox, Aileen, *South West England 3,500 B.C.–A.D. 600.*
Usherwood, *Patterns of the Past.*
Collingwood & Myres, *Roman Britain and the English Settlement.*
Pearce, Susan M., *The Kingdom of Dumnonia.*
Baring Gould & Fisher, *Lives of the British Saints.*
Boggis, *History of the Diocese of Exeter.*
Smith Dorrian, *Historical Records of Church and Parish.*
Kyrton, *Crediton.*
Ormerod, *Archaeology of Eastern Dartmoor.*
Porter, H. M., *The Celtic Church in Somerset.*
Seebohm, *Evolution of the English Farm.*
Chanter, *Christianity in Devon before A.D. 909.*
Vivien's Visitations.
Victoria County History of Devon.
Place Name Society, *Place Names of Devon.*
Poole, *Domesday to Magna Carta 1087–1216.*
Postan, M. M., *Essays on Medieval Agriculture and General Problems of the Medieval Economy.*
Denman, D. R., *Origins of Ownership.*
W. Country Studies Library, *William Harding Thompson Survey.*
Bishops Registers.
Clarke, *The History of Tithes.*
Hoskins, *Devon.*
Francis Osborne, *The Churchwardens Accounts of Chagford.*
Snell, L., *The Suppression of the Religious Foundations of Devon and Cornwall.*
Francis Osborne's notes.
Lewis, *The Stannaries.*
Pennington, *Stannary Law.*
Pearce, Tho., Gent, *The Laws and Customs of the Stannaries.*
Hatcher, John, *English Tin Production and Trade before 1550.*
Broughton, D. G., *Tin Working in the Eastern District of the Parish of Chagford, Devon.*

Risdon, Tristram, *Antiquities of Devonshire.*
Marshall, *Rural Economy of the West of England.*
Whiddon, Helen, *Whiddon of Novia Scotia.*
Prince, *The Worthies of Devon.*
Public Record Office, *Inquisitions post mortem.*
Snell, F. J., *Devonshire: Historical, Descriptive, Biographical.*
Lethbridge, Sir Roper, *Hands across the Sea.*
Polwhele,
Swete,
Lysons,
Blundell's Worthies.
Harris, H., Industrial Archaeology of Dartmoor.
Dartmoor: A New Study.
Chagford Parish Magazines.
Tithe Commutation Map.

INDEX

Okehampton, 17, 18, 67, 69, 71, 72, 105, 106, 129
Orchard, 103
Orchard Cottage, 16, 97
Orchestra, 79
Organ, 34, 78, 113
Ormerod, 11, 110, 111, 117
Osborne, 122, 125
Outer Down, 44

Pack-horses, 85
Padley, 16, 51, 58, 94, 129
Parish Council, 129
Parish Nurse, 120
Parish Magazines, 110
Parliamentarian, 67-72
Parliament of Tinners, 39, 45
Parochial Church Council, 129
Parsonage House, 33, 51, 73, 76
Patron of the living, 29, 30, 33, 36, 59, 73, 75, 82
Peasants Revolt, 23
Penny Readings, 112
Perkins, 76
Perambulation of forest of Dartmoor, 23
Perrot, 109, 128
Perryman, 94, 95, 110
Pews, 78
Phillpotts, 121
Phoenicians, 38
Pillars, 31, 78
Ploughs, 14
Plymouth, 67, 69, 71, 127
Plympton, 22, 69
Poddicomb, 34
Polewhele, 21
Police force, 108
Ponte de, 18
Pony sale, 129
Population, 23, 90, 127, 129
Poor, 34, 53
Post Office, 90, 108, 121
Pottery, 3
Pounds, 5
Prestonbury, 5
Princetown, 91, 117
Propogating the Gospel, 64
Protestantism, 32, 33, 36, 74
Protestation Returns of 1642, 96, 98, 99
Prouz, 20, 21, 24, 30, 49, 50, 55, 87, 88, 92, 94, 97
Pulpit, 124 *see also* Restoration of Church
Puritan, 64, 67

Quarters, the Four, 32, 52
Quintatown, 104, 105

Railway, 106, 109, 117
Raleigh, Sir Walter, 46, 49, 54, 57
Reading Room, 111, 120
Rectors, 36, 103, 104
Rectory, 31, 76, 77, 78, 79, 80, 90, 113
Reed, 107, 108, 121, 125
Reformation, 49, 54
Refugee Committee, 122
Register, 34
Restoration of Church, 78
Restoration of King, 84, 90
Rioting, 23, 31
Ring of Bells, 89, 107, 109
Risford de, 20, 92
Roads, 34, 52, 88, 90, 106
Roman, 5, 6, 8, 12, 18, 29, 38, 39
Roman Altar, 113
Romano-British, 13
Rome, Church of, 29, 36
Roodmas, 44
Round Pound, 5
Rowe, 51, 87, 94
Royalist, 67-72
Royal Oak, 89
Rugg, 58, 95
Rushford Manor, 6, 12, 16, 19, 20, 35, 43, 50, 52, 68, 77, 82, 87, 90, 92, 104, 105
Rushford Barton, 16, 50, 77, 97
Rushford Bridge, 19, 52, 105
Rushford Mill, 16, 77, 85, 97, 105, 121, 127
Rushford Wood, 16, 50, 77, 94

Saint Katharine, 32
Saint Katharine's House, 32, 33, 34, 51, 94
Saints—stores and altars, 32, 42, 43
Salisbury Plain, 3, 4
Sandy Park, 105
Sandy Park Mill, 19, 85, 97, 126
Saxon, 7, 8, 10, 13, 29, 39
School, 78
School Fees, 111
Schooling, 110
Scorhill, 4, 121
Scott, 107
Scutt, 87
Seale-Hayne, 82
Seaward, 96
Second World War, 127, 128
Seymour, 61, 88
Seynthill, 94
Shaft Mining, 40, 45

LIST OF SUBSCRIBERS

F. A. Allanson
R. F. Allen
Edward & Miranda Allhusen
Dracaena Allhusen
Gwyneth Amery
Major A. A. Anderson, B.A.
Yvonne St. Claire Anderson
M. Andrews
Deidre, Carrol & Patrick Anketell-Jones
Joyce Annear
Surgeon Captain R. G. Anthony, R.N.
Michael Aplin
David Ashby
Mrs. Jean Awdas
W. & E. Avery
Dorrie Davey Baker
Julian & Barbara Baldock
Mrs. Marjorie Banks
Bath University Library
Joan Bayliss
Peter Beach
Vivienne Beddoe, M.B., B.Chir.
S. J. Bedford
Mr. & Mrs. N. A. Beer
Jane Beeson
Mark Beeson
Sue Bizley (Bullers Arms)
Mrs. K. M. Blower
Dr. & Mrs. K. W. Bolt
John Bosanko
Evan & Su Bowater
Mr. Leonard H. Bradbeer
Drs. Nick & Mary Bradley
P. B. Brailsford
Miss V. B. Brimblecombe
Mark & Janet Brimicombe
June Bohannan Brown
Mr. Christopher Bulley
The Rev. W. J. Bulley, Rector of Chagford
Alfred Burgess
K. J. Burrow
B. Butler
Pat Butler

Mr. & Mrs. D. V. Cannon
Felicity Capper
Chagford Parish Council
Chagford Primary School
Chris Chapman
Mrs. M. E. Cheshire
Mrs. H. Clark
Mr. K. W. Clarke
John Somers Cocks
R. G. Collins
Bernard Collop
Charles Cooper
Peter Cooper
Lucinda Cork
C. A. L. Cornick
Dr. F. H. Cotton
Audrey E. Cottrell
William C. Cousens
Mrs. J. V. Cowderoy
Miss M. E. Croft, M.R.C.V.S.
C. A. H. Croxford
David Cuss
C. E. N. Deane
L. S. L. Deas, Dowlais
Mrs. Dorothy Debenham
B. & M. Denham
Devon Library Services
Devon & Exeter Institution Library
Gerald & Margaret Lethbridge Dicker
G. E. Diggines
Barbara Y. Dixon
Mrs. Timothy Dudgeon
Keith Eddey
Mrs. J. Edmonds
David Edmund
Gilbert J. Ellis
J. M. Elsworthy
D. L. Endacott
Mr. Lewis Endacott
Paul Endacott
C. T. Every
Exeter Rare Books
Mary & Donald Eyles

141

Gillian & Grant Fear
V. M. Fearne
A. & W. R. Fitzpatrick
P. Fitzpatrick
S. Flexman
Joel Fisher
S. P. & F. G. Ford
Sheila & Stanley Ford
Keith Stephen Fox
Mr. & Mrs. K. Frankson
P. A. French
Wendy & Brian Froud
The Geisinger Family
Sidney Godolphin
Genia Goelz
K. Goodridge
Mrs. W. T. Goodwin
Mr. & Mrs. Jonathan Greene
Lucille Greenfield
Thomas A. P. Greeves
Grace Griffin (née Swaddling)
J. Lloyd Griffith, F.R.C.S.
F. G. Hammett
C. F. Hankin
Pamela Harrison
David J. Hawkings
R. G. Haynes
Richard Hayter, Esq.
Anne L. Hayter-Hames
Belinda Hayter-Hames
Eric Hemery
Mr. & Mrs. Anthony Hill
Mr. & Mrs. M. L. Hill
Major Andrew Lloyd Hill, R.T.R.
Dot Hills
Dr. Hans Hollander
J. Holmes
Ms. A. R. & T. E. Hood
Mrs. M. E. Hooper
Mr. & Mrs. J. W. Hornby
Eleanor Mary Howarth
James Howlett
P. W. Hughes
Mr. & Mrs. Christopher P. Humphries
Margaret C. Hunt
Tom Hutchings
Elizabeth A. Jarrold
J. Loveys Jervoise
Captain P. N. Jones
Mary Shaw Jones
Miss S. H. Jones
Jill Jory
Graham Joyce
Caroline Kalberer

Jean A. Kellaway
Frances & Patrick Kenna
Elmfield Guest House, Moreton Hampstead
W. Kraak
Miss Rosemary Knight-Bruce
Mr. & Mrs. B. Knox
Miss Ruth Lake
Mr. & Mrs. L. M. Lees
Mrs. P. F. Lester
Dr. & Mrs. D. A. Lewtas
Stephen Lewtas
Mr. & Mrs. J. F. Lindsay
D. Luscombe Lobb
Mr. L. D. Lucas-Endacott
Mr. E. W. Luscombe
David & Geraldine McPhie
George Maddaford
James Maggs
Sylvia Mallett
Ian & Marcia Mallinson
Douglas B. Marsh
Commander E. D. Marston
Ms. Lucy MacKeith
Michael Masterman
Mrs. M. Lucy May
W. Matthews
J. E. Maxwell-Hyslop
Avril R. Meredith
Avril Meredith
Brian Le Messurier
J. R. Middleton
G. A. Miller
Mrs. M. G. Morgan
David Morgan
Mrs. G. P. Mortimore
Peter & Mary Morton
David Nation
Miss D. E. B. Newcombe
Jill Nicholson
Mrs. Julie North
Cyril W. Northcott
Michael & Penny O'Connor
Mr. T. H. O'Dell
Hugh Daniel Osborne
John Mardon Osborne
Laura & Michael Osborne
Mary B. E. Osborne
Winifred Osborne
Joyce Packe
Penelope & John Parsons
Mrs. A. B. Palmes
Miss M. M. Paterson
Mary Payton
George Collins Peacock

Violet L. Peacock
Steven & Katharine Pefanis
Mary Pennington
A. E. McR. Pearce
S. B. Perigal
Andrew & Michaela Perryman
Philip & Gillian Perryman
William & Annette Perryman
Paul Pettit
Pamela M. Phipps
Mrs. Jean M. Phillips
Graham Pidgeon
M. E. P. Piercy
C. D. Pike, O.B.E., D.L.
Mary Plunkett
Arthur M. L. Ponsonby
Christopher W. Pote, F.R.I.C.S.
Ann Powell
Joan Powell
Douglas Price
Graham Price
Susan & Nigel Price
Elizabeth Prince
Laurie Pritchard
John Proudlock
Mr. F. T. Prowse
N. V. Quinnell
Mrs. Muriel Reson
Edgar Rice
E. H. Reynolds
Ethel W. Rice
Iain & Rosalind Rice
Iain Rice
Laurence C. Rice
Roger L. Roberts
Rusty Rose
R. A. Sampson
Robert F. D. Sampson
Virginia Sandon
Denis Sargent
Richard Sawers
Wm. A. Saxton
Mr. H. S. Scawen
Gilbert H. W. Scott
Tomás O'Seanacáin
Mary Christine Seiles
Joyce Sillem
F. H. Smardon
Leonard E. Snowden

Dr. Christopher C. B. Southgate
Mr. & Mrs. David G. Spear
M. Spiller
Mr. & Mrs. J. G. Stanford
Mr. F. H. Starkey
Margaret E. Stead
Thelma M. Stephens
Mr. & Mrs. Alan Stevens
Mrs. M. Stevenson
Alan Stone
Leonard Stone
Martin C. G. Stone
Mrs. R. J. G. Stone
Marjory Jeanette Stuart
Mr. Michael Stubbs
Dr. & Mrs. T. D. V. Swinscow
K. W. Switzer
Peter D. Symons
W. P. M. Telfer
D. L. B. Thomas
Richard & Christina Thomas
Robert Hole Thorn
George & Patricia Thurlow
C. L. Tompson
Torquay Natural History Society
Elizabeth T. Tucker
Christabel Tunnington (née Prouse)
Jock Tweedie
D. Underhill
Mr. R. J. P. Underhill
M. Underwood
Allen Van Der Steen
Richard Waller
Enid Watkins
D. A. Watson
Ellen Webb (née Painter)
Margaret Webb
Margaret L. Weeks
Mrs. Pamela Weeks
Mrs. Angela Wells
Miss K. Wells
John B. Whidden
G. H. Whitley, Esq.
Gladys Williams
R. N. Wills
J. F. R. Withycombe, M.Chir., F.R.C.S.
The Rev. Geoffrey Wrayford, M.A.
Michael Wreford
John Young